Henry Hudek

CARDINAL RULES of INVESTING

It's Not Too Late To Retire A Millionaire

KNOWLEDGE BUREAU
NEWSBOOKS

WINNIPEG, MANITOBA, CANADA

ISBN 1-897051-34-4

Printed and bound in Canada

Canadian Cataloguing in Publication Data

Hudek, Henry 1951-

Henry Hudek Cardinal Rules of Investing it's not too late to retire a millionaire –2005 ed.

Includes Index
ISBN 1-897051-34-4

1. Retirement wealth planning –Canada – Popular works. 2. Retirement planning – Canada – Popular works. I. Title. II. Title: Cardinal Rules of Investing

HJ4661.3212 2005   343.7105's   C2005-900153-4

Published by:
Knowledge Bureau, Inc.
Box 52042 Niakwa Postal Outlet, Winnipeg, Manitoba R2M 0Z0
204-953-4769 Email: reception@knowledgebureau.com

Editorial Assistance: Joan Homewood, Northbridge Publishing
Front Cover Artwork: Ray Phillips
Back Cover and Page Design: Doug McArthur

To my parents, Ed and Chris Hudek, for the fantastic beginning, the embracing family and the constant enthusiastic support.

TABLE OF CONTENTS

CHAPTER 4   61
Putting the Rules Into Practice

CHAPTER 5   73
Building A Cardinal Portfolio Today

CHAPTER 6   91
Who Is This Clark Kent?

TABLE OF FIGURES

Appendix I

Re-Thinking Your Investment Strategy For Retirement

I have been investing in stocks since 1977 and fascinated by financial markets since the sixties. An avid reader of the financial press and any books on investing I can understand, I thought I knew my stuff. With an undergraduate degree in Economics, an MBA in the mid-1970s and a CFA in the mid-1990s, I was educated to the hilt. I performed corporate strategic planning, marketing administration and trade negotiating during the eighties and nineties, and I counseled institutional and private clients throughout the last decade. I was also an officer and director of research for a national Canadian mutual fund dealer for almost ten years, as well as serving on the Board of Directors.

I was lectured to, cajoled, seminared, and marketed to by what seemed like almost every portfolio manager and mutual fund company in Canada. In the process I became fairly cynical about the whole business of money management. It seemed that so much of the business was marketing and hype, and so much of the media coverage was sensationalized fear mongering.

At the same time, I saw that many individual investors were lost in equity investing. They were dependent on advisors, who are increasingly and constantly pressured to follow the "hot" products that are promoted by the financial services industry and played up in the media. A dispassionate, rational approach to equity investing is almost impossible with the amount of marketing that goes into Technology funds, Far East funds, Health Care funds and other flavour-of-the-month funds and stocks. The need to have advertisable products leads many investment managers (or mutual fund manufacturers) astray. The 'thrill of the hunt' makes investors forget that real, long-term success in investing comes from discipline, from consistency and from conservatism, not from seeking the latest 'next best thing'. Such an environment makes us forget that it's not the new hot sectors that make the money. It's not the fads. Forget flavour-of-the-month. Vanilla and chocolate, properly executed, are the only flavours most investors need. Anything else stems from greed, and that's downright dangerous for mature clients approaching retirement.

Then I found Cardinal Capital Management. Cardinal's performance record — with annual average returns in excess of 17% over the twelve years since it began, even through the crash of 2000-2001 — was a wake-up call. Do you know that over twelve years, a 17% annual return turns $150,000 into $987,000, even without adding any more cash? Cardinal's extraordinary track record grabbed my attention and dragged me back to the basics, back to what I call the Cardinal Rules; these are the investment principles followed at Cardinal Capital Management, the principles that lead to such success. If Cardinal had been better known over the past decade, there would be many more Canadians retiring happy millionaires today, instead of exchanging worried looks over investment statements and deciding to postpone the retirement plunge. This book is a story of these principles, where they came from, how they work, why they work, and how you can use them to build a millionaire retirement plan.

As we close in on retirement, we need to save more and invest better to ensure we attain the prosperity and comfort we seek for our retirement years. We need the premium return that equity markets offer, but we need to avoid being burned by the well-known fires of those same markets. The Cardinal Rules, as practiced by Cardinal Capital, will help you to do just this.

Because of our strong belief in the Cardinal methodology, and its demonstrated success in managing risk while generating healthy returns, my company, Value Partners Investments, has chosen to bring Cardinal Capital to retail investors. In the past Cardinal has served only institutional and high net worth investors. Value Partners Investments Inc. was created to provide a mechanism for the smaller investor to access Cardinal expertise, cheaply and smoothly. I am a part owner and an employee of Value Partners. The company paid for the writing of this book because we firmly believe that all investors should have the opportunity to realize the rewards of prudent investing without the gut-wrenching fears that can come with equities. This is especially important for those of us nearing retirement, who need to grow our portfolios relatively safely, free from the whims and ambitions of the wizards of Wall Street or the titans of Toronto.

We hope that this book will give you a thorough understanding of the Cardinal Rules, so that you can be proactive in realizing your investment dreams. Whether working with a broker, financial advisor or managing your own investments, this book will explain an investment approach that can have a dramatic result on the amount of wealth you build in your investment portfolio. I hope you enjoy learning about the Cardinal Rules and that you benefit from knowing them.

And, if you catch the bug as I have, feel free to spread the word.

Henry Hudek
October 2005

CHAPTER ONE

Old Enough For Smart Investing, But Wise Enough To Worry About Risk

Ain't it great getting older? Yes, the back hurts and I feel tired more often, but the foolish, frantic antics of youth are behind me, and I can look with some satisfaction on my life up to this point. Many Canadians have reached, or soon will reach, that certain stage in life where these may be their sentiments. They have twenty or thirty years of employment behind them, the kids are leaving home, the mortgage is under control, and they find themselves facing the next stage of their lives. I hit that point a while back and it was a bit of a wake-up call.

Like me, many Canadians have finally accumulated a little cash, even if it's only in RSPs (Retirement Savings Plans) and is not quite enough to retire on. But it's a start. Now retirement and the "golden years" are staring us in the face and we know, way down in our gut, that the little voice we've heard in our heads for the last decade is right — "It is time to get serious about a retirement plan."

With so many Canadians facing this challenge it's not surprising there is a boom in the number of articles being published and seminars available on how to plan for your retirement. Bookstore shelves groan under the weight of advice books on how to get rich and how to invest your money. Unfortunately, most of the "experts" advise you to start saving in your twenties and to max your RSP contribution every year. That of course is great advice, but where were they when I was twenty-five? It's too late now for me to start early!

THE BENEFITS OF MID-LIFE INVESTING

The good news is that it's not too late. You can start now, in mid-life, and still build a comfortable, prosperous retirement. In fact, some might even argue that this is an excellent time to get started. You are probably in your peak earning years and your household expenses may be declining. Your house may be paid for or you may be considering downsizing. Your kids may have left home — along with the considerable expense of camp fees, tuition, hobbies, etc. — and you may be moving to a smaller vehicle or from two cars to one. Also you probably have a better handle on your expenses than you had in your thirties or forties.

The most significant point in all this is that you may now find that you have more disposable income to invest in your retirement. What you do with that money now can have a dramatic effect on how soon you can retire and your retirement income when that time comes. So is there a secret you need to know at this stage?

If you are like most Canadians, your retirement nest-egg is now invested largely within your RSP, haphazardly bought year after year, usually in late February. As an investment advisor I often saw investors with a mish-mash of mutual funds (with the occasional GIC thrown in for good measure), which are often near duplicates and occasionally address contradictory investment needs. If there was a financial advisor involved, there was often an attempt at maintaining a certain foreign/Canadian balance and a reasonable asset allocation. Often the total was just what could be saved-up from year to year on an ad-hoc basis, rather than the result of a long-range savings goal.

You should congratulate yourself on building a sizable nest-egg already, but now is the time to focus on that "millionaire retirement." To carefully turn that nest-egg into a significant retirement fund you now have to consider investing more in the stock market, and investing in a more directed way. It is definitely time to put together a retirement plan that assesses how much income you expect to need and identifies where it's going to come from. This will tell you how much more you need to save, and how aggressive you have to be with your stock market exposure.

PERILS AND PITFALLS OF EQUITY MARKETS

Whoa! Back up that train! STOCK MARKET EXPOSURE?! We've all read about those nefarious stock promoters, insider trading, management lay-abouts, hostile takeovers – all sorts of dastardly deeds to be concerned with. And everyone will tell you there are no guarantees with the stock market. Your money is at risk there! The stock market may be okay for those who would rather gamble than invest, but this is my retirement money we're talking about, not some spare cash. Is that really a wise place to invest the money that will support me throughout my retirement?

Investing in the stock market can be so dangerous that it's terrifying for many to consider. Remember Nortel, Canada's biggest company in early 2000? Nortel was a cover success story for *Business Week* magazine in August of 2000 and many assumed it was a respectable company priced somewhere near reasonable value. Yet its stock price dropped like a proverbial stone after August 2000, falling from $124 to $45 in a matter of weeks (and near $10 by the end of 2001). When the tech bubble burst, the TSE Index, which peaked in August 2000, fell for two consecutive years, closing in September 2002 with a loss of 39% (see **Understanding Equity Indices**, pg. 4). That means every $10,000 invested in the Toronto equity index in August 2000 had fallen to a value of $6,100 by September 2002.

And, you've heard of Enron, of course. It's a nasty word now, but in its heyday, Enron was ranked by *Fortune* magazine near the top of its "Most Innovative Companies" list six years in a row. It was named one of the five most admired firms in America! How could so

In order to compare equity markets to each other and to other investments, such as bonds, financial analysts needed something to act as a proxy for the markets. As a benchmark, financial analysts invented an "Index" for each stock market, which is composed of a selection of stocks traded on that market, chosen to represent the diversity and make-up of the entire market, but using a smaller universe of stocks. These stocks are usually the more common and larger stocks (by market valuation) whose behaviour is believed to mirror the behaviour of the market as a whole.

There are many such indices, because there are many equity markets. New York has the S&P 500 and the Dow Jones Industrial Index, London has the Financial Times Stock Exchange (FTSE), Frankfort has the DAX, and Paris has the CAC. Toronto's largest stocks are represented by the TSE 60, and the overall market is proxied by the S&P/TSX Composite. The EAFE Index is designed and managed by Morgan Stanley Capital and represents the Europe, Australia and Far East regions — that is, all non-North American, supposedly developed economies. If North America is added back in, one gets the World Index, also prepared and managed by MSCI.

Analyzing the historical behaviour of these indices gives us some insight into how big the equity premium is market to market, and relative volatility between markets. Indices are also often used as benchmarks against which investment managers are measured. If it were physically possible to buy all the stocks in the index, without incurring the fees and commissions involved, then it follows that if you were hiring an investment manager, you would only be happy with one who could pick stocks for you that "beat the index." Until recently it was too difficult or expensive to buy the index, so comparisons of the performance of the index to a manager was only meaningful if you measured the manager before the deduction of all fees and costs. Now there are Exchange Traded Funds, which have drastically reduced the cost of buying all the stocks in the index, so it is physically possible for an investor to "buy the index," making comparisons on an after-fee basis practicable. Too often, however, one finds comparisons of the fee-free index made to the after-fee results of a manager, which of course, makes the manager look worse by comparison.

many supposedly knowledgeable people be so drastically wrong?

Nortel and Enron are not the first examples of popular delusion in stock market pricing, nor will they be the last. Decade after decade there is a disintegration of some supposedly perfect company, either after deliberate wrongdoing or after some terrible miscalculation. Details unfold slowly but inexorably, like some ghastly flower in the sun, until all the sordid facts lie strewn across the headlines. The results are always disastrous for the thousands of poor souls who thought they had found the end of the rainbow only to discover that their pot of gold had evaporated before their eyes. These are searing reminders of how expensive an investing error can be, and it should make prudent folk raise an eyebrow and think.

Huge declines in certain stock prices happen continually. Large declines in the overall market happen regularly. Some investment managers even boast that they love it when the market goes down because it gives them a chance to buy stocks cheaply. That may be acceptable (if painful) for young or rich investors, but for those of us who are retired or plan to retire within ten or so years, our investment portfolio must provide a reliable income. We can't afford to sell our stocks at bargain basement prices just because the markets decide to be down for a few years.

THE STOCK MARKET PAYOFF

There is no question that skepticism and cynicism about the stock market is warranted. Equity investing does have its pitfalls, and it can be a very scary ride. Yet everyone says that over the long term, investing in equity gets rewarded (which by the way is absolutely true). Over the long term, equity markets have always provided a risk premium return over investments in fixed income securities. Studies going back to neo-industrial England support that contention and studies of more recent times in the U.S. reinforce it. Investing in equities makes more money – OVER THE LONG TERM.

It's just too bad that we are now living in that dang short-term! I've got to start taking out money soon, and I don't want to be forced to do it when my portfolio is down 15%! Yet if I want to realize the gains I need for a wealthier future, I need to have some proportion of my investable assets invested in equities. If only there was a way to smooth out the roller-coaster ride so that we could reap the gains of equity investing without the stomach-churning dips and plummets frequently associated with the equity markets. What's a person to do?

That's why I needed to write this book. Too many investors are terrified of the stock market, yet almost all of us need the benefits that investing in equities can and should provide. Investors, especially those concerned about having portfolios safe enough to generate a retirement income, need to know about better ways to invest in equity markets.

Reducing the Risk – The Cardinal Rules

And there are actually better ways. In fact, you could have done quite well investing in Canadian equities even in the bear markets of 2000 and 2001. Remember those two years from August 2000 to September 2002 when the average $10,000 turned into $6,100? How would you like to have made 18% instead? I know of someone who actually turned every $10,000 in Canadian equities that he managed into $11,800 over that period. This fellow, Tim Burt of Cardinal Capital Management in Winnipeg, manages money for institutions and private clients. Tim uses some basic rules and strategies for equity investing that you too can follow to keep your money growing consistently, even during turbulent times. I call these the Cardinal Rules and I believe that they are a set of the most important investing tactics that exist. Some of Tim's clients have actually become quite wealthy through his money management, but that's not the focus of his strategy. Tim's Cardinal Rules are designed to provide a good return while keeping your money relatively safe; anything beyond that is just fortuitous.

The success of Cardinal Capital Management speaks to the strength of the Cardinal Rules. Cardinal Capital beat the TSE index handily, even though the index is a fiction free of all fees and costs. This out-performance is not only along the dimension of rate of return, which everybody cares about, but also along the dimension of volatility, which everyone should care about.

The Cardinal Rules are not really new, but they are continually forgotten, and so become new over and over again. There is enough in this book to guide dedicated do-it-yourself investors, who have the inclination, the aptitude and the time to run their own portfolios, into the habits and process they will need to be successful investors. For the rest of us, *Cardinal Rules of Investing* lays the groundwork needed to work with our financial advisors to develop and implement an investment strategy that will help us reap the rewards of equity investment, while minimizing the risk.

The enthusiasm I feel for the Cardinal Rules is like the gospel to an evangelist. Over the years I've met many wonderful people who do not deserve the investing experience they are getting. They need to know about the Cardinal Rules. Even if they do not execute them personally, they need them as a shield against the daily expositions and the breathless marketing spiels that abound in the media. The Rules give a context, a grounding, to help us resist the enticements and manipulation that we see around us. Learn them, remember them and use them to judge all you hear and see in your investing endeavours. The confidence you gain will help you move from the sidelines of the equity market into investments that will truly help you build a wealthier retirement.

CHAPTER TWO

Calm and Profit
In the Midst of the Storm

The period from 1993 to 2005 produced many financial nightmares and a number of mind-numbing, gut-wrenching outcomes. The human mind is a wonderful thing; it can forget all sorts of bad stuff. But remember when the Canadian federal government deficit was out of control and the loonie fell to 63 cents US? Remember Bre-X showing the world that Canadian mining expertise was second to none on the planet? Remember the implementation of the Euro, and the European Monetary Union in January 1999? Remember Y2K threatening to stop international economic activity dead in its tracks? I've mentioned the Nortel collapse, but do you also remember the bond market collapse as interest rates rose in February 1994?

At the time, each of those events caused reverberations in the equity markets and in each of those cases individual investors suffered tremendous angst and turmoil as they struggled with their choices and decisions. In 1994, a series of fast and furious interest rate hikes caused the Canadian stock market to fall 12% from February through June. In November the Mexican peso crisis caused the EAFE index to fall in value by over 8.5% through February 1995. The Russian ruble crisis of 1998 caused the Canadian index to fall by 25% from May

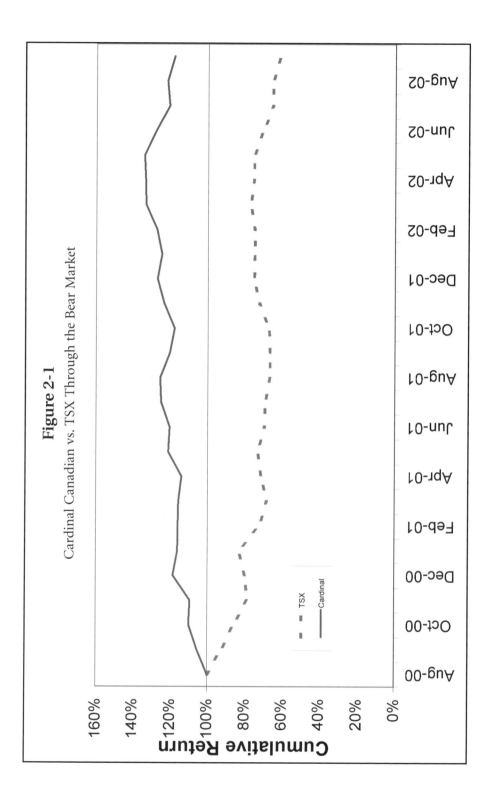

Figure 2-1

Cardinal Canadian vs. TSX Through the Bear Market

through August. And the events of September 11th 2001 caused the EAFE to fall 10.3% and the S&P 8% that month. On top of this the bursting "tech bubble" exacerbated the ongoing free fall of most of the world's major indices. Our memories blank out a lot of the difficulty investors experienced in making investment decisions when faced with these events, but tribulations and turmoil are the stuff of equity investing. It is painful at the time, even though after the fact the decisions may seem relatively obvious. If you are like me, you would rather avoid the turmoil, but you need the returns.

Being active in financial planning and investment research over these tumultuous years I saw client after client panicked and dazed by these events. Even experienced professionals were looking over their shoulders, wondering what was going to hit them next. And yet throughout this period Cardinal Capital Management's returns outperformed the major indices.

HOW CARDINAL RULES DECLAW THE BEAR

Not only did Cardinal reap better returns than the indices, but it also had a generally much smoother ride. Even during the difficult period from August 2000 to August 2002 when the TSX cumulative return declined 39%, Cardinal was up 18% (see Figure 2-1).

In the five years ending March 2005, Cardinal Capital had annual average returns over five times that of the TSX index, with only two-thirds of the volatility (see *Understanding Volatility*, pg. 14-15). Year after year their Canadian and foreign portfolios turn in stellar results in terms of extra returns. Figure 2-2 shows how Cardinal's Canadian and Foreign portfolios grew from their inception till 2005, despite the bear market of 2000-2002. This figure graphs how $10,000 invested in a Canadian portfolio at Cardinal in 1993 would have grown to $55,610 by 2005, and $10,000 invested in Cardinal's Foreign portfolio in 1995 would have grown to $35,952 by the same date. The 10-year average annual return for the Canadian Cardinal portfolios was 18.7% versus the Canadian market index which aver-

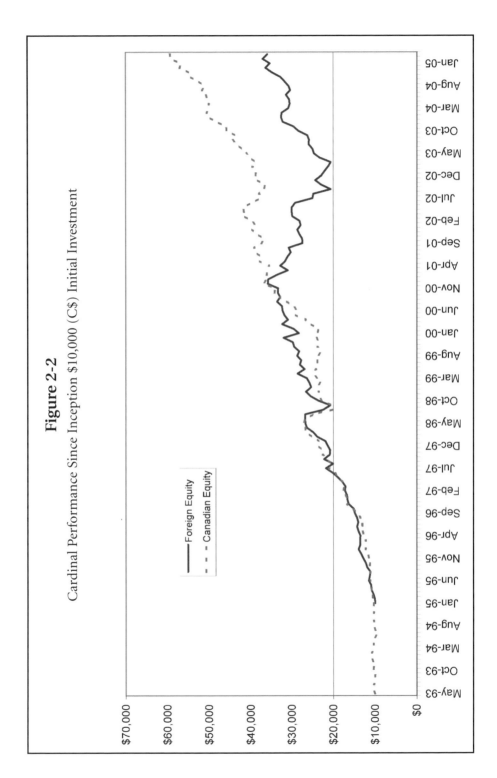

Figure 2-2

Cardinal Performance Since Inception $10,000 (C$) Initial Investment

aged 11% per year. This means that while the $10,000 invested with Cardinal turned into $55,610, in the TSX that $10,000 would only have grown to $28,389.

Cardinal's investment strategy is built on the Cardinal Rules — rules which are based on well-established principals of value investing (see *Understanding Value Investing*, below), a school of investing established by Benjamin Graham and made popular in recent years by Warren Buffett.

Value investors have a saying: Don't think of it as a stock market; think of it as a market of stocks! If one stops to think and really understand that point, it is a very enlightening and liberating

---

UNDERSTANDING VALUE INVESTING

Value Investing is a strategy of stock selection that was first delineated in the writings of Benjamin Graham and David Dodd back in 1934. In summary, the strategy consists of establishing a conservative value for a business and then only buying when the business can be bought for significantly below that conservative value (in order to establish a margin of safety.) Because the important part of the process is establishing the value of a business, the strategy depends heavily on extensive fundamental analysis of the business, including its assets less liabilities and its future earning power. In all cases, conservatism is used in this valuation, with no regard for speculation about growth from new products, new markets, new technologies or whatever. What is proven by historical results is given substantial weight and what is speculative, or unproven, is ignored or given far less credence.

The second element of the strategy is buying at below value. The amount below value is established as a margin of safety because, theoretically, if the price is significantly below real value, it is less likely for the price to fall further, thus protecting the investor's principal. The assumption behind the strategy, of course, is that value is independent of the market's price for the company and that the market will at some point irrationally value a business lower than its real value.

concept, if a little cryptic. What they are saying is that you don't have to buy the entire stock market. The stock market is like a supermarket that you can browse through, check out the selections and compare the prices. If you see something you like, you can buy it. If you don't see anything you like, you can come back tomorrow, or the next day. The stocks will still be there, although probably at new prices. You can't predict the prices, but the point is that you never have to buy a stock at a price you don't want to pay.

GETTING A SMOOTHER RIDE

We all know the stock market at times seems to make no sense, with

UNDERSTANDING VOLATILITY

There is a truism about investing that if you take big risks, you qualify for bigger returns. But what is risk? Financial analysts, in their wisdom, have generally settled on volatility of returns – that is, how much returns go up and down over any period of time — as one way to define risk in investing. It is not the only way, and may not be the best way, but it is an informative measure.

Equities are a volatile asset class, meaning that if you look at monthly returns of a stock market index, you will see that those returns vary widely, as much as 10 – 20% in some months, both positive and negative. On the other hand, GICs are at the safe extreme in terms of asset classes, with monthly returns that are always the same and absolutely predictable (as long as the issuer stays solvent).

It is interesting to note that the return for GICs does not include any variation in the capital value. All of the return on GICs is comprised of interest, which is only true because there is no market for GICs. If there were a daily market and regular quotes, then GICs would vary in value just like bonds do, where prices fall as interest rates rise, and vice-versa. It is because of this that volatility of returns for bonds is lower than for stocks but higher than GICs. Because there is a bond market and prices are available daily, the monthly return for bonds consists of the interest, plus or minus an adjustment for change in capital value. Bonds do go down in value, but if one ignores the daily changes in values changing drastically over a month or even a week. At times, certain stocks are bought and sold for prices having little relationship to what they are really worth. Individual stock prices can be influenced by rumour, by marketing pitches, by patriotic emotions, or any number of other factors. If it's the hot stock that everybody wants a piece of . . . it's probably overpriced. If it's a stock that has been promoted in the press and subject to a brokerage marketing blitz . . . it's probably overpriced. Yet these stocks may be included in the index that describes the overall stock market's behaviour, and they help to make up the rough road that we see reported in the headlines. Unfortunately too many investors, influenced by the financial media

UNDERSTANDING VOLATILITY (CONTINUED)

capital value and focuses only on the guaranteed maturity amount, they behave just like GICs.

A statistical measure for volatility of a series of returns is the standard deviation, which conceptually, is a measure of how much the returns vary from the average return. This treats returns below the average the same as returns above the average (although arguably, returns above the average do not mean extra risk to the investor). An investment with an average return of 1% per month (12.7% per year compounded) might have a standard deviation of 4.5% per month which means that on an investment of $100,000, you would make an average of $1,000 per month, but that monthly returns will mostly vary (67% of the time) between a loss of $3,500 and a gain of $5,500 ($1,000+/-$4,500). In this example it is theoretically possible for one month's return to be three standard deviations below the average or -$12,500. ($1,000-$13,500) The calculation is a statistical one, which means it is subject to the limitations of statistics. The most common failing in the use of standard deviation is that the value is not meaningful unless there are at least 30 observations from which to do the calculation. If one is measuring monthly returns, 30 months of observations means that at least a 2-1/2-year history must be available or the conclusions are not valid. If annual returns are being measured, 30 years of history are required.

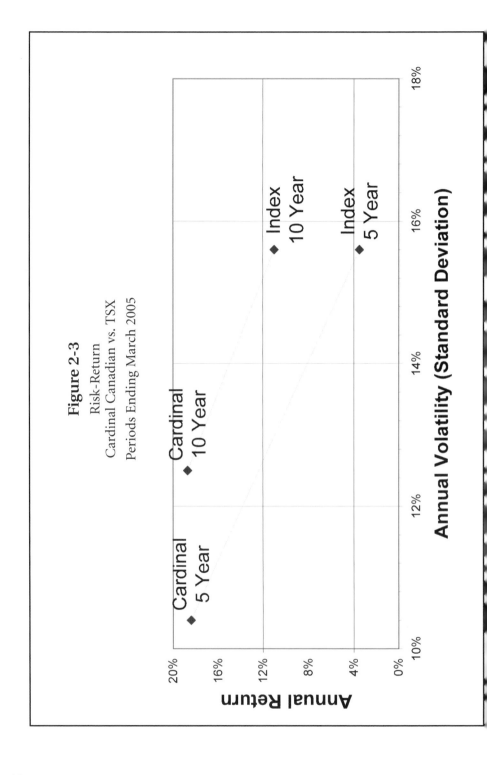

Figure 2-3
Risk-Return
Cardinal Canadian vs. TSX
Periods Ending March 2005

and the advertising of the investment industry, approach the stock market like a teenager out shopping; they feel they absolutely have to buy the latest hot stock or support the trendy soon-to-be-great company. But it doesn't have to be that way.

This simple concept is at the heart of the Cardinal Rules. You don't need to buy the whole market. The stock market may be a rough road, but you don't need to drive through the ruts and potholes that are part and parcel of the whole market. You can choose instead to buy stocks that act like shock absorbers on your portfolio. If you don't buy the inflated price stocks that make up part of the market, presto! . . . you'll have a smoother ride than the market in general. And, if you only buy high quality stocks, and buy them only when they're cheap, poof! . . . an even smoother ride. The Cardinal Rules help to ensure that smoother ride by helping you pick shock-resistant stocks for your portfolio that will give you a smoother ride without sacrificing the performance that makes for good returns.

This is illustrated in Figure 2-3 in what we call a Risk-Return Chart, which plots the annual returns of a portfolio against the volatility of returns. The chart shows that for the last five years, the index for the Toronto Stock Exchange (a good proxy for Canadian equities in general) had an average annual return of about 4% and an annual volatility of about 15%. So what does an annual volatility of 15% mean? An annual volatility of 15% represents a monthly standard deviation of about 4.5%. This means that almost all of the time (99%, according to the statistics) the return in any one month can vary by as much as three times the monthly standard deviation, or about 13% from the average monthly return. Therefore, on a $100,000 portfolio, you could see values fall (or grow) up to $13,000 in a month. That's a fairly rough ride, but pretty typical of equity investments. The rate of return for the index of 4% (see Figure 2-3) is lower than the historical average for equities because it reflects only a five-year period, a period that includes the years 2000 and 2001

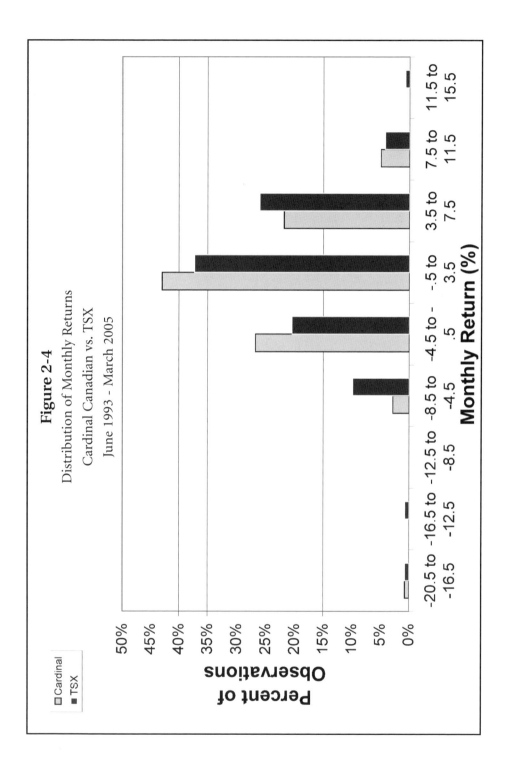

Figure 2-4

Distribution of Monthly Returns

Cardinal Canadian vs. TSX

June 1993 - March 2005

when stock values plummeted. More importantly, you can also see that the Cardinal Canadian portfolio's performance over the same period had a volatility near 10% indicating significantly lower risk, and the average returns were higher, at about 19% per year. Similar results are apparent from the 10-year history, although here the TSX returns are much closer to their historical pattern, returning an annual average near 12%.

So how did the Cardinal Rules protect a portfolio so well through one of the most tumultuous investing periods in the last thirty years? Figure 2-4 shows the distribution of monthly returns on the TSX index against the distribution of returns on the Cardinal Canadian portfolios. This chart reflects data for returns over 142 months from June 1993 through March 2005. Each column shows where the rate of return in each of those 142 months fell for both the index and for the Cardinal portfolios. For example, the tallest column shows that in about 37% of the months, the return for the TSX fell between -0.5% and 3.5%, whereas for Cardinal 43% of the months fell into that range.

This alone indicates that the Cardinal average monthly return is likely higher than the TSX. However, the really important differences are in the tightness of the distribution. More of the Cardinal months were closer to the midpoint than for the TSX. True, the Cardinal portfolios never had a month over 11.5%, as the index did, but Cardinal also had no months in the −12.5 to −16.5% bracket and it had two-thirds fewer months in the −4.5 to −8.5% bracket. In general the Cardinal portfolio results are much more concentrated and closer to the centre of the distribution. That's the definition of a smoother ride; smaller and fewer bumps. A necessary corollary of less variation in the monthly returns is that a Cardinal portfolio is likely to have fewer great months, as well as fewer terrible ones.

"OK," I hear you saying, "So I get a smoother ride. But why is that important if in the long term everything turns out all right?"

For investors who have the stomach to see their portfolio go down by as much as 15% in a month that may be alright. But many of us, especially those of us nearing retirement, are depending on our portfolios to provide an income in the near future. For us a 15% decline could be disastrous, because we don't have time to wait for it to grow back again.

WHY MARKET FLUCTUATIONS CAN REALLY HURT

You may have heard of dollar-cost averaging. That's where you deposit a certain amount of money every month, for example, to purchase an investment that fluctuates in value. This is a good strategy because when the investment fluctuates down in price, your regular deposit will buy more shares in the investment. But what happens if instead of depositing or buying an investment, you are selling in order to take out a regular amount of cash each month, as you will need to do when you are retired? Let's take a look at an example. Figure 2-5 is a classic retirement planning spreadsheet showing a $500,000 portfolio for a person aged 65 who hopes to withdraw $34,000 per year from the portfolio. The anticipated growth rate for the portfolio is 6%, a reasonable estimate. The table shows that the money lasts till age 100 at which time there is only $23,517 left. But what about fluctuations? This spreadsheet assumes constant 6% growth. The only investment I know with a smooth growth rate is a GIC and last time I looked GICs weren't paying 6%, especially if you want annual interest.

Now let's take a look at how a share price might look over the same period if it had an average growth of 6%, but was subject to market fluctuations. Figure 2-6 shows two columns of share prices, one with a constant annual increase in share price of 6% which shows that a $10 share will grow in value to $81.47 in the 35 years. (I love compounding!) But of course, we all know stocks don't behave that

Figure 2-5
Retirement Planning
Constant Growth Rate

Age	Beginning Portfolio	Annual Growth 6%	Annual Income	Ending Portfolio Value
65	$500,000	$30,000	$34,000	$496,000
66	496,000	29,760	34,000	491,760
67	491,760	29,506	34,000	487,266
68	487,266	29,236	34,000	482,502
69	482,502	28,950	34,000	477,452
70	477,452	28,647	34,000	472,099
71	472,099	28,326	34,000	466,425
72	466,425	27,985	34,000	460,410
73	460,410	27,625	34,000	454,035
74	454,035	27,242	34,000	447,277
75	447,277	26,837	34,000	440,113
76	440,113	26,407	34,000	432,520
77	432,520	25,951	34,000	424,471
78	424,471	25,468	34,000	415,940
79	415,940	24,956	34,000	406,896
80	406,896	24,414	34,000	397,310
81	397,310	23,839	34,000	387,148
82	387,148	23,229	34,000	376,377
83	376,377	22,583	34,000	364,960
84	364,960	21,898	34,000	352,858
85	352,858	21,171	34,000	340,029
86	340,029	20,402	34,000	326,431
87	326,431	19,586	34,000	312,017
88	312,017	18,721	34,000	296,738
89	296,738	17,804	34,000	280,542
90	280,542	16,833	34,000	263,374
91	263,374	15,802	34,000	245,177
92	245,177	14,711	34,000	225,888
93	225,888	13,553	34,000	205,441
94	205,441	12,326	34,000	183,767
95	183,767	11,026	34,000	160,793
96	160,793	9,648	34,000	136,441
97	136,441	8,186	34,000	110,627
98	110,627	6,638	34,000	83,265
99	83,265	4,996	34,000	54,261
100	54,261	3,256	34,000	23,517

Figure 2-6
Share Price Projection

Age	Annual 6% Growth	Fluctuating Market
65	$10.60	$10.00
66	$11.24	$9.00
67	$11.91	$8.00
68	$12.62	$10.00
69	$13.38	$12.00
70	$14.19	$14.00
71	$15.04	$16.00
72	$15.94	$18.00
73	$16.89	$20.00
74	$17.91	$15.00
75	$18.98	$14.00
76	$20.12	$15.00
77	$21.33	$20.00
78	$22.61	$23.00
79	$23.97	$25.00
80	$25.40	$27.00
81	$26.93	$24.00
82	$28.54	$22.00
83	$30.26	$26.00
84	$32.07	$32.00
85	$34.00	$35.00
86	$36.04	$38.00
87	$38.20	$44.00
88	$40.49	$46.00
89	$42.92	$44.00
90	$45.49	$40.00
91	$48.22	$49.00
92	$51.12	$50.00
93	$54.18	$55.00
94	$57.43	$60.00
95	$60.88	$67.00
96	$64.53	$63.00
97	$68.41	$62.00
98	$72.51	$68.00
99	$76.86	$77.00
100	$81.47	$82.00

way. Their price goes up, their price goes down. The second column in Figure 2-6 shows the share price in a fluctuating market.

Figure 2-7 shows the same data in a line graph. You can clearly see that the lines end up roughly at the same spot, but one was a nice smooth ride, which doesn't happen in the real world of stocks, and one bounced around on its way up. Note that the fluctuating share price starts out with a dip, but by age 71 it is back above the constant growth price. There are periods where it's below and periods where it's above, just like the real world that we hate so much. By age 100 let's say the market has priced the shares at $82. In the long-term we've achieved our 6% growth. According to the retirement plan, everything should be hunky-dory, right? We should have enough money to last to age 100.

It's true that in both cases the value grows from roughly $10.00 to roughly $82.00 in 35 years, but the difference is in how the unavoidable fluctuations affect the ending value when you are taking out a regular income, as demonstrated in Figure 2-8. When the investment fluctuates down, we have to sell more shares in order to get the same income. If it drops a lot, we might have to sell a lot more

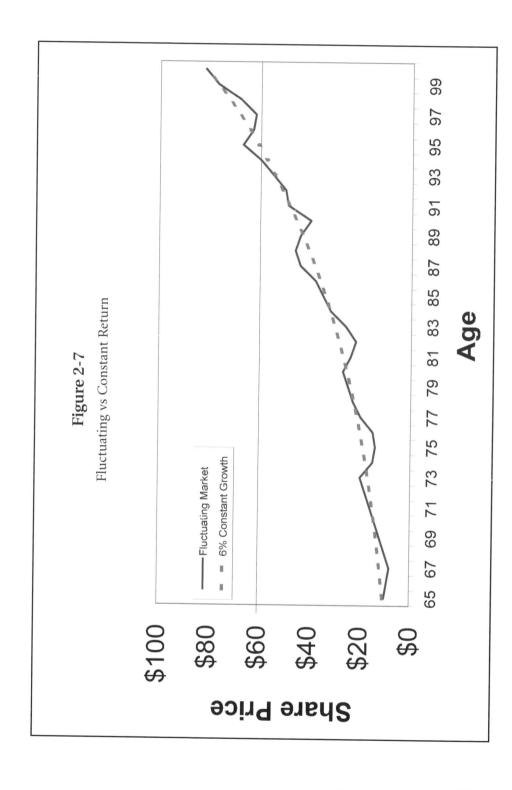

Figure 2-7

Fluctuating vs Constant Return

Figure 2-8

Retirement Planning
Fluctuating Growth Rate

Age	Share Price	Value Opening Portfolio	# of Shares	Annual Income	# of Shares	Value End Portfolio	# of Shares
65	$10.00	$500,000	50,000	$34,000	3,400	$466,000	46,600
66	9.00	419,400	46,600	34,000	3,778	385,400	42,822
67	8.00	342,578	42,822	34,000	4,250	308,578	38,572
68	10.00	385,722	38,572	34,000	3,400	351,722	35,172
69	12.00	422,067	35,172	34,000	2,833	388,067	32,339
70	14.00	452,744	32,339	34,000	2,429	418,744	29,910
71	16.00	478,565	29,910	34,000	2,125	444,565	27,785
72	18.00	500,136	27,785	34,000	1,889	466,136	25,896
73	20.00	517,929	25,896	34,000	1,700	483,929	24,196
74	15.00	362,946	24,196	34,000	2,267	328,946	21,930
75	14.00	307,017	21,930	34,000	2,429	273,017	19,501
76	15.00	292,518	19,501	34,000	2,267	258,518	17,235
77	20.00	344,690	17,235	34,000	1,700	310,690	15,535
78	23.00	357,294	15,535	34,000	1,478	323,294	14,056
79	25.00	351,407	14,056	34,000	1,360	317,407	12,696
80	27.00	342,799	12,696	34,000	1,259	308,799	11,437
81	24.00	274,488	11,437	34,000	1,417	240,488	10,020
82	22.00	220,447	10,020	34,000	1,545	186,447	8,475
83	26.00	220,347	8,475	34,000	1,308	186,347	7,167
84	32.00	229,350	7,167	34,000	1,063	195,350	6,105
85	35.00	213,664	6,105	34,000	971	179,664	5,133
86	38.00	195,064	5,133	34,000	895	161,064	4,239
87	44.00	186,495	4,239	34,000	773	152,495	3,466
88	46.00	159,427	3,466	34,000	739	125,427	2,727
89	44.00	119,973	2,727	34,000	773	85,973	1,954
90	40.00	78,158	1,954	34,000	850	44,158	1,104
91	49.00	54,093	1,104	34,000	694	20,093	410
92	50.00	20,503	410	34,000	680	-13,497	-270
93	55.00	-14,847	-270	34,000	618	-48,847	-888
94	60.00	-53,287	-888	34,000	567	-87,287	-1,455
95	67.00	-97,471	-1,455	34,000	507	-131,471	-1,962
96	63.00	-123,622	-1,962	34,000	540	-157,622	-2,502
97	62.00	-155,120	-2,502	34,000	548	-189,120	-3,050
98	68.00	-207,422	-3,050	34,000	500	-241,422	-3,550
99	77.00	-273,375	-3,550	34,000	442	-307,375	-3,992
100	82.00	-327,334	-3,992	34,000	415	-361,334	-4,407

shares and before you know it, we're out of shares to sell. Instead of your portfolio lasting till you're 100, it runs out early! The expanded Retirement Planning spreadsheet in Figure 2-8 takes into account fluctuating share prices. Instead of the money lasting to age 100, the market fluctuations have hurt and at age 91 we have only $20,093 left — not enough for another year's income. People depending on fluctuating equities who need income late into their nineties are in trouble. Of course, the converse is also true. If prices rise, we will have to sell fewer shares and our money will last even longer. The long and short of it is that we can't afford to take a chance on the rough road with our retirement nest-egg; we want to have a smoother ride but we still want, and need, to earn the level of returns the stock market can offer.

A smoother ride is not the whole story of course. A smooth ride is precious for those of us who are approaching the time when we will need income from our portfolios. We want to have fewer bumps so that when we pull out income from our portfolio, it's not at the expense of selling securities at fire-sale prices. There's no doubt that GICs will give you a great, really smooth ride. However, GIC returns are pretty low (awfully close to the rate of inflation). If you're like most folks and you want to live better than your current savings will allow, you really need a better rate of return than GICs. That's why we have to be in equities in the first place and why shock-resistant stock picks are crucial.

A SMOOTHER RIDE CAN STILL PAY

Figure 2-3 demonstrated that the shock-absorbers work, but not at the expense of returns. In fact, over the life of Cardinal's Canadian portfolios, the average monthly return for Cardinal was 1.33% while the index was only 0.95%. I know this difference doesn't seem like much. However, when compounded over 142 months, that seemingly minor difference represents growing $1,000 into $5,926 from June 1993 to March 2005 in the Cardinal case versus only $3,300 with the index. Think of it this way. Investing $1,000 in May 1993 with Cardinal earned you an average $34.69 per month for 142 months whereas the same $1,000 in the TSX only earned an average $16.20 per month.

You can see that as well as being safe the Cardinal portfolio record on returns is no slouch either. We can get the benefit of equity returns, even with a lower risk (some would say "boring") portfolio. That's a lot more attractive to me than a get-rich-quick approach, and it should be an attractive goal for all investors nearing retirement.

NOT ONLY IN CANADA, YOU SAY?

These Cardinal Rules work not only in Canada, but in the international arena as well. The Cardinal foreign portfolios also have racked up returns significantly higher than the market indices. Compared to the EAFE, an index that measures how equities in developed economies outside North America perform, Cardinal's foreign (non-U.S.) equity portfolios managed using the Cardinal Rules have generated exceptional returns over the past twelve years. When measured in US$, the EAFE returned 4.1% per year, whereas the Cardinal portfolios (in US$) returned an average of 13.7% per year. This performance (which "smoked' the index) did however come at the cost of extra volatility.

Even the S&P 500 in the U.S. had a three-year return of only break-even to March 31, 2005, versus the Cardinal U.S. portfolios which averaged over 6% per year for the same three years, with only two-thirds of the index's volatility. The Cardinal Rules make money!

RESISTING THE HIGH-FLYERS

Some might sneer at returns of only 6%, such as Cardinal delivered on U.S. equities, but that is where danger lies. Greed in investing is a disease that makes for a rough ride. It's an emotive word with negative ethical connotations, but in the context of investing it simply describes that natural human desire to get as much as you can for your efforts. In this instance, we might also be driven by our competitive instincts to try and outdo our peers. But, if you want to enjoy the smoother ride promised by the Cardinal Rules, you must ignore the temptations of high returns. Ignore the media's focus on the latest hot stock and investment industry promises of amazing per-formance. Ignore the chatter from your colleagues about their latest coups. (Funny how they don't bring up their disasters as often, although they are inevitably there.) There will always be products with high recent rates of return, like technology stocks in 1999. (That's one reason why mutual fund companies have so many prod-ucts; there's always something out there with recent high returns that can be advertised.) Unfortunately, rarely does the same investment continue to have the same stellar returns, and buying the hot or heav-ily promoted investments usually results in buying closer to the peak than the bottom.

Resisting greed generally pays off. Consider the Cardinal Canadian equity portfolios in the early years, from June 1993 through May 1998. Cardinal did start off slowly. In the first year the market moved up 14%, while Cardinal rose only 3%. After three years, the market was up 45%, or 13.1% per year compounded — a good run for the markets. The Cardinal portfolios, in contrast, were up only 30%, for an average annual compounded return of only 9.2%. Impatience, greed or just plain cussed human nature could have had us pounding on the doors at Cardinal whining about why our returns were not as good as the market, but remember, we want the smoother ride. We want and need the safety that the Cardinal Rules can give us. And come to think of it, 9% is not a bad return – if we could average that for the rest of our lives, we would be in pretty good shape.

As events unfolded in the Cardinal case, it actually turns out that things did get a little better. The years 1996 and 1997 were won-derful for the markets. The markets gained 22% each year, but Cardinal picked up two wonderful years averaging 44% each year. Over Cardinal's first five years, when the average annual return for the market was 16.8%, Cardinal's was 22.1%. Ten thousand dollars invested at inception for the five years ended May 31, 1998, would have grown to over $27,000 at Cardinal as opposed to $21,700 in the market index, and it was safer too. Cardinal's returns were 13% less volatile than the index!

Generally, a shock-absorbed portfolio will not beat the index when the market is up to its usual silly valuations. However, over time it appears that the shock absorbers don't cost you much in the way of returns. The 10-year average return for the Cardinal Canadian portfolios was 18.7% ($10,000 turned into $55,610) whereas the TSX index averaged 11% per year ($10,000 turned into $28,389). If the Rules can deliver results like this maybe it's time we looked at them in more detail to see how we can internalize them and then use them in our investing lives.

CHAPTER THREE

The Cardinal Rules of Conservative Investing

The Cardinal Rules are twelve simple, practical rules that should help you grow your portfolio without experiencing the nerve-wracking torment of major fluctuations in value that are experienced by the markets in general. These rules are intuitive and obvious. They rely on the principles of value investing espoused by the likes of Warren Buffett and Benjamin Graham. Sometimes it may seem that the rules are so simple they should go without saying. But history shows that time and again, investors forget them, markets go wild, and people get hurt. Memorize these rules. Chant them as a mantra. Use them as a shield to protect you from the media and market hype. Make them your friends. Even if you never intend to be your own stock-picker, you should understand and approve the strategy that you want to be used in managing your hard-earned wealth.

The Cardinal Rules – Summarized
1. Buy Quality
2. Buy Value
3. Be Patient
4. Use Common Sense

5. Don't Over-diversify
6. Hold Winners, Sell Losers
7. Emphasize Liquidity
8. Avoid Market Timing
9. Reinvest Income
10. Build Wealth
11. Stay Balanced
12. Don't Overtrade

Pretty logical, right? It certainly sounds straightforward, but let's dig into each rule to get a better understanding.

The "Big Two" Rules – Buy Quality and Buy Value — generally deal with two elements of investing, the what and the when; what to invest in, and when to do it. Some of the Rules are more important than others and some are more complex, but the first two will have the most immediate impact on your success. The rest of the Rules are important for longer-term success and generally deal with how you manage your portfolio, even after you have selected your first stocks.

RULE #1. BUY QUALITY

That sure sounds easy, but what is quality? With respect to stocks the principle concept here is conservatism. Look for historically profitable companies that have a record of rewarding shareholders with a share of the profits through dividends (see *Understanding Dividends*, pg. 32-33). Look for companies with an understandable business model and an advantage in their existence, be it strong brand image, market dominance, barriers to competition or a resource/technology advantage. Choose conservative, established companies with a solid financial structure. A solid financial structure means not too much debt on the balance sheet and a good history of generating free cash flow.

Look for solid dividend history

A long, solid dividend history is really helpful. Many studies emphasize the value of selecting stocks using dividend yield as a criteria. James P. O'Shaughnessy's groundbreaking book, *What Works on Wall Street* (McGraw Hill, New York, 1998, pg. 144) identifies choosing the fifty highest-dividend yielding stocks from what he described as the Large Stock universe as a strategy that does "almost twice as well as their universe with virtually the same risk." He also points out that this strategy results in a maximum loss much less than that experienced by Large Stocks as a whole. His methodology looked at all liquid U.S. equities with a market capitalization of $150 million or more (in 1998 dollars), and defined Large Stocks as those whose market capitalization exceeded the median market capitalization for the group.

A study called "A Yield Effect in Common Stock Returns" by J. Grant, published in the Winter 1995 issue of the *Journal of Portfolio Management*, concludes: "High dividend yielding stocks of both small and large firms were the best performing equity investments for the thirteen-year period ending in December 1992. . . . High-yield portfolios earn abnormally high rewards in the presence of relatively low return standard deviation." In other words, high returns with low risk — investor nirvana.

Jeremy Siegel's latest book, *The Future for Investors* (Crown Publishing Group, New York, 2005, pg. 244) strongly recommends sustained high-dividend yield as a criteria in stock selection based on his studies of data from 1957 to 2003. He also points out that the criterion appears to work even in the international arena. Referring to a study in the U.K., he states: "[The] highest dividend yielding stocks in the U.K. outperformed the lowest-yielding stocks, just as I found for the United States. The divergence was substantial, amounting to 3 percent per year over the past 103 years."

Therefore, look for companies with a healthy record of dividend growth and where the payout ratio (dividends/net income after tax) is low enough that the dividend appears protected and where future growth in dividends appears likely. Dividends are how investors make a regular cash return on their investment. If this cash stream is growing, all the better. In fact a growing cash stream does more than return more cash; it generally boosts the share price as well. The example of the Royal Bank and its growing dividend described in the next chapter and detailed in the Appendix I is a strong case in point. Dividends are probably the most helpful indicator there is of which stocks to select in using the Cardinal Rules.

UNDERSTANDING DIVIDENDS

Companies are in business to make a profit for their owners, their shareholders. These owners are individuals or RRSPs or institutions like charitable foundations, pension plans, insurance companies or government funds like the WCB. When companies are new and generally faster growing, all the profits they make usually need to be reinvested in the company to support its growth. However, as companies mature, become larger and more profitable and opportunities for growth are fewer, they often do not need all the profit for reinvestment and can pay some of it out to shareholders in what are called dividends. In doing so, management is recognizing that their shareholders have invested in their shares to earn a return and they should be rewarded for this and for sticking with a company over the long haul. Dividends demonstrate that management knows profits do not belong to management, but to shareholders.

When profits are partly paid out as dividends, the proportion of profit paid out is called the Payout Ratio. Management generally do not like to reduce the dividend being paid, so they usually establish a regular dividend rate that they believe can be sustained yearly into the future. As profits grow, companies will generally increase their dividend, so that a record of dividend growth is established. But because high payouts generally mean reduced growth, management must walk the fine line between increasing dividends (higher payouts) and increasing profits (lower payouts). In the past it has been a regulatory requirement that many pension plans, insurance companies and government funds invest only in companies that have an established dividend history. In fact, because for many years almost

Most importantly dividends tell us something about a company, and they tell us more reliably more so than the earnings statement and the balance sheet can tell us. Neither dividends nor dividend growth are subject to the discretion of accounting treatment. They are a fact that cannot be manipulated or exaggerated. The company must have the earnings and the cash to pay the dividend. As Jeremy Siegel states: "…dividends are a critical ingredient in generating trust between shareholders and management and confirming management's statements about earnings" (*The Future for Investors*,

UNDERSTANDING DIVIDENDS (CONTINUED)

all companies paid dividends, that was the chief source of return for investors. Capital gains were an almost incidental occurrence. In more recent years, however, many companies that are striving for rapid and continued growth have paid no dividends, despite very healthy profitability. It has become common for portfolios to hold no dividend-paying stocks and to depend on capital gains as the entire source of returns.

When looking at dividend-paying stocks, one variable to consider is the Dividend Yield. This is the annual dividend amount divided by the market price and can be considered analogous to a coupon yield on a bond, even though it is not guaranteed and the stock price (principal) can vary significantly. A high dividend yield indicates a higher return is available in the form of the dividend, making total return less dependent on the potential capital gain.

A newer form of higher-yielding equity much in the news lately is Trust units. Because dividends are taxed twice under the traditional corporate structure, once when the company earns them and again when the investor receives them, trusts have been created to take over operations of low-growth, high-dividend payout firms. Unlike companies, trusts are not taxed on those earnings that are distributed to the owners of the trust. Therefore trusts (be they royalty trusts, business trusts or real estate investment trusts) should generally be considered to be like other businesses, except with high payout ratios. The sustainability of the dividend (distribution) is the key concern, which goes to the source of the earned cash and to the business model. Yield alone is insufficient as criteria for selection.

pg. 133). The presence of dividend growth is a signal that management has substantial confidence about the future. It also demonstrates management is considering the shareholders and their return rather than assuming the right to control (and possibly squander) the free cash flow generated from company activities. If you worry about the recent issues raised about corporate governance and accounting debacles (and you should) then dividend history and dividend policy are a solid way to be reassured about the reality of a corporate situation. On top of all this, a company's management does everything it can to avoid the stigma of cutting dividends.

There can be no doubt that dividends are a wonderful thing, which is why they are such a crucial element in the Cardinal Rules definition of Quality. The effect they have on a portfolio is substantial. Dividends help anchor a stock's value, stopping it from fluctuating as drastically as many other stocks in the market, and they offer the added benefit of compounding if they are re-invested in the portfolio. In other words, dividend-paying stocks are effective shock absorbers for a portfolio. This is great news for those of us approaching the income-from-our-portfolio stage. But that's not the best news about dividends. When a dividend is increasing, it is even more potent.

Some academics argue that the dividends a company pays may actually hurt its growth prospects. Theoretically, dividends mean there is less cash available to re-invest in growing the company. So why would we look for dividends? Because dividends are a return of cash on our investment and because dividends send a message. Dividends are a sign that management has substantial confidence about the future they can foresee, and a growing dividend means that management is confident in growing earnings. Dividends are a direct message to investors.

To understand how important dividend yield is in maximizing returns from investments over the long-term, consider the cases illustrated in Figure 3–1, showing a high yielding (4%) dividend growing at 10% compared to a lower yielding dividend (1%) growing at 20%. On a $100 initial investment, by year eleven, the 4% dividend is now yielding over 10% of good solid income, while the low yield stock is still only paying 6%. In fact, the faster-growth dividend stock does not pass the slower one until year seventeen, and seventeen years is a long time to wait and be at risk. Yes, the higher-growth dividend stock might get more capital gains for us over the long term, but again, that's only speculative. A cheque in the hand is proof that cash from the company has gone to you. No doubt about the amount. There is no creative accounting in the dividend such as might happen on an earnings statement. With the Cardinal Rules we crave security, and we get it from higher current yields, not from potential growth or arbitrary accounting treatment.

Consider the Financial Structure

Buy Quality also means looking for a solid financial structure. In particular, this is reflected in the amount and cost of debt used in the corporate structure, along with the quality of the assets. Is the company highly leveraged so that 70% of its assets were bought with debt, or do interest and bank charges (as well as Obligations Under Capital Leases) eat up a huge part of the gross income of the firm? Is the firm vulnerable to increasing interest rates on its debt, either because large portions of debt are in demand form or because significant amounts mature in a relatively near term? Look at the debt/equity ratios and the interest coverage ratio. Ben Graham used to focus on net working capital, and while opportunities that meet his criteria appear to be long gone, the analysis still provides useful information about the downside risk in a firm's balance sheet. Assets with a large component of real estate are often understated on a balance sheet, and cash, marketable securities, or good accounts receivable are attractive elements in the corporate structure. A close look at a business's financial statements (see *Understanding Financial Statements*, pg. 38-39) will provide you with all kinds of valuable information in assessing financial structure.

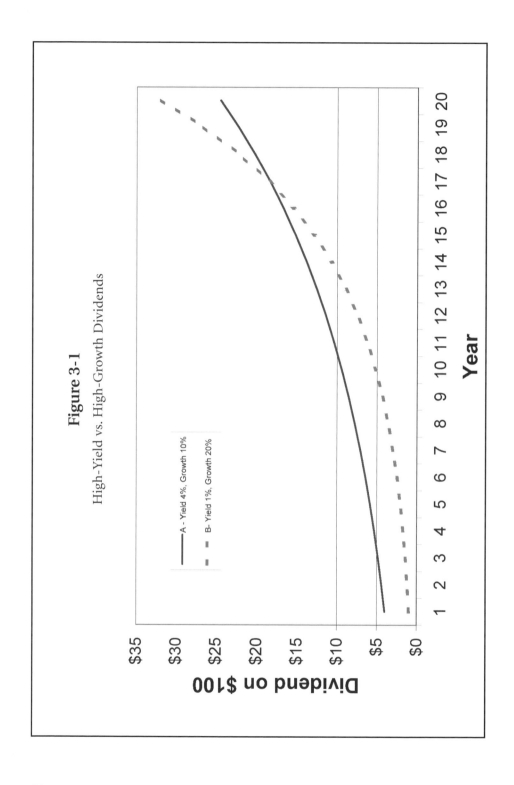

Figure 3-1

High-Yield vs. High-Growth Dividends

A - Yield 4%, Growth 10%

B - Yield 1%, Growth 20%

Dividend on $100

Year

Examine the Fundamentals

Buy Quality means not buying hot or trendy stocks, even though there may be an aura of quality surrounding them. Look beneath that aura of quality for companies that have a dominant, well-established brand and a significant market share. Look for solid business franchises with compelling business fundamentals. The buzz-phrase for value investors is "sustainable, competitive advantage." That's what we are looking for. Quality companies have a clear business model, uncluttered with technological issues, that makes sense to you as a consumer and as an investor. Do you know if there are people out there who need to buy the firm's product? If you were such a person, do you understand why you would choose that company's product? In considering quality, imagine what Warren Buffet or even old Ebenezer Scrooge would think. Would he want a company whose business model he couldn't understand? Would he want a highly leveraged company that had only recently turned its first profit? Would he want a management who was sitting on a huge cash position with no sign of handing anything back to shareholders in the form of dividends?

Is There Free Cash Flow?

The reason we look at free cash flow instead of earnings is because free cash can be returned to the investor, whereas with earnings, that's not necessarily so. In a high-growth, capital-intense industry, all earnings may need to be re-invested just to keep up to the competition, so the cash flow from operations is not available to be distributed. High maintenance, reclamation or exploration costs can encumber a firm's cash and prevent the company from paying it out to shareholders, which in the end, is what an investor wants.

Buying Conservative

Conservative "quality" stocks may not make exciting cocktail conversation, but thousands of Canadian bank shareholders can attest that

Companies need cash to operate and to build their infrastructure and their asset base. That cash generally comes from three sources: shareholders, banks or government, with shareholders being the most frequent. That's because most banks and governments won't loan or grant cash to a company unless there is first a significant contribution by shareholders in the form of equity. As a business grows and demonstrates profitability banks are more prepared to loan it money, and that's where danger comes in. Banks generally offer loans on terms that are pretty lucrative for the bank; they minimize the risk of their loans by encumbering assets and restricting dividends. In general, for accepting a business's risk they compete with its shareholder for the business's free cash. The Balance Sheet (or Statement of Financial Position) will show how big the debt is (sum of Long Term Debt, Long Term Debt Due Within One Year, and Other Loans) compared to the Shareholders' Equity (perhaps including Deferred Taxes as noted below). In considering Quality, debt/equity should be less than 1.0 or should not be large in comparison to its industry peer group. Large, growing debt may demonstrate a company's success, if that debt is being investing wisely in rapid growth. Unfortunately, it also increases the riskiness of the business, and as soon-to-retire investors seeking security, risk is not something we want to pack into our portfolios.

The Notes to the financial statements will have a schedule of debt maturities and interest costs and rates. Is the debt staggered in terms of maturity so that the company will not be renewing too much of it at once? If much of the debt matured at one time that creates the risk that the company may be forced to accept high interest rates at renewal. Does a lot of the debt mature soon? Is it at interest rates that are much lower than rates currently prevailing, which would mean that the company will likely have higher interest costs in the near future. In general, think of the company's debt as you would approach your mortgage. Is there an acceptable or unacceptable level of risk in the terms and situation the firm finds itself?

Interest and Lease Payments have a prior right to corporate cash flow over shareholders. In fact, banks get downright ornery when they don't get their money, and can start making demands or threatening bankruptcy. That generally is not good for shareholders.

Therefore look on the Income Statement to see how the sum of Interest and Lease Payments compares to Gross Income. If a large portion of the debt is in Loans, this generally means that the rate is floating. If interest rates were to go up 1%, how much would interest costs go up? How about 2%? Would there still be ample Gross Income to pay taxes and preferred shareholder dividends as well as leave some left over for the common shareholder?

The cushion for debt is the Retained Earnings portion of shareholders' equity on the balance sheet. This represents an accumulation of past profits not paid out as dividends. In a mature firm, this can be a significant part of the overall capital, which can be a good thing for reducing downside risk in a firm. Retained earnings belong to shareholders and can be used by the firm to carry them through unprofitable periods. When matched with a significant cash position or high Current Assets, it means that a significant part of the value of a share in the company is fairly readily liquid and can be used to increase dividends or buy back shares. Therefore, high Retained Earnings or a high Net Working Capital (Current Assets less Current Liabilities) can indicate a business with an attractive financial structure.

Government cash in most Canadian corporations comes in the form of Deferred Taxes. Usually this cash is not subject to immediate demand and has arisen from depreciating assets on the balance sheet more slowly than tax legislation allows. Complexities aside, this cash can often be added to Shareholders' Equity in determining debt to equity. The company will generally be able to keep it as long as they operate.

year-in, year-out dividends and modest growth will really beef up a portfolio. Occasionally I hear investors complain that their portfolios don't have anything different in them, just boring old banks, insurance companies and blue chips. There's nothing wrong with that, especially if you can buy them at the right price. When you are building a secure retirement you don't want companies that are in the headlines; you just want your money to grow.

RULE #2. BUY VALUE

Not only do you want to buy conservative stocks, you want to buy them only when they are cheap. Stocks go through cycles fairly frequently. If you look at any stock quote on-line or in the press, you'll usually find the 52-Week High and Low. Even for the most conservative, "boring" stocks this range is often amazingly wide — from 20% to 25%. For more exciting, but still conservative stocks, the range can exceed 100%. And for speculative stocks, which under Rule #1 should be avoided, the High can be several times that of the Low. Often investors will look at this range and buy stocks with wider ranges, believing this is indicative of how much money they can make. Avoid this trap. Use the low end of the range to start assessing when a stock might be attractively priced. Just think, if you can buy a stock near the bottom of its annual range, at some point within the following year, that stock may well be worth from 20% to 25% more! Value is best determined by analyzing a number of financial ratios, including its historical price/earnings (P/E), its price/book value (P/BV) and its price/cash flow (P/CF) (see *Understanding Financial Ratios*, pg. 42-43). This is where applying the Cardinal Rules can get onerous because this detailed analysis can take more time and effort than many of us are willing to expend. However, if you are willing to commit the time to develop these ratios and compare them with those of other companies in the same industry, you can obtain the knowledge you need to Buy Value. Look to buy when these ratios are at or near historic lows or when the ratios are lower than those of their peer group. By doing this and by avoiding stocks where these ratios appear overvalued or where they are setting new highs, we know we are buying value.

THE CARDINAL MINDSET

Rule #3 is the start of a series of rules that don't deal with the what and when to buy; but instead with the how. They deal with behaviour and attitude, which over the long haul are the more important elements of being successful as an investor. Your behaviour and your mindset are more likely to determine your success than any one specific trade (although of course, your trades are determined by your attitude).

RULE #3. BE PATIENT

If you want to buy Quality stocks but find that the ones you have identified are running up in price or appear expensive at this point in time, do not succumb to the concern that the stocks are "getting away from you and must be chased." Be patient. A buying opportunity will come when the market gets bored with these stocks and the prices slide back.

I'm told there is a Taoist concept in Chinese called Wu Wei, which means "to act without taking action." In managing a portfolio, doing nothing is not really doing nothing. It is letting the portfolio do its work, letting the natural course of events unfold. Don't be panicked into buying at expensive prices. Similarly, don't worry if your stocks don't go up in value or even go down immediately after you buy them. Bad news in the media can make the market nervous and depress your stock price even further. If you have bought wisely, have confidence in your decision. If you believed the stock was good value when you bought, why not buy more after there has been an earnings disappointment or a broker downgrade? In recent markets such events have often severely impacted price in the short run, because most investors focus on only one quarter at a time. But often the news does not relate to the long-term health or success of the company. Be patient – Wu Wei.

If you have chosen wisely and feel you own a piece of a good company, then who cares that the market sees it differently? As we've seen, the market ain't all that smart! There is a lot of short-term volatility and the media is full of reasons for it. Every day the market index moves with stories about inflation fears, deflation fears, interest rate fears, political tension, etc., etc. None of this matters in determining whether you want to keep or sell a stock. Ignore it. Once you've picked and bought a stock, then own it. Take pride in it. You've got a piece of the economic engine that creates goods and wealth for the people of the globe. Be a fan, not a faddist!

UNDERSTANDING FINANCIAL RATIOS

Financial analysts have a whole set of criteria through which to judge the value of stocks. Some of the most common ones are P/E, P/CF, P/BV and P/EG. Data for these come from the financial statements of the company as well as from the stock market. The "P" is the current market price of a share, and the denominators come from the financial statements — "E" is the earnings per share (eps). Therefore a share priced at $10 with achieved earnings per share of $2 in the last fiscal year has a P/E of 5 (10/2). Because these earnings are calculated after-the-fact, this is often called P/E (Trailing). For many companies, financial analysts calculate projected earnings per share based on expectations for the current fiscal year. A P/E calculated using this eps is called the P/E (Forward) or Prospective. Since the market generally anticipates the future, most analysts prefer the forward-looking number. Traditionally value investors have tried to "normalize" eps by looking at extraordinary items, average historical eps, growth rates in eps, and data from corporate statements. This can result in a conservative projected long-term eps that would be used in the P/E ratio. Using a consensus of analysts' opinions does not tell the investor how conservative or how normalized the projected eps is and that is why, under the Cardinal Rules, it would be better to develop this material oneself.

BV is an abbreviation for Book Value, which comes from the company's Balance Sheet or Statement of Financial Position. In the Balance Sheet, all the assets of the company are totaled, as are all of its external liabilities. Usually assets are greater than these liabilities and what is left over is the value of the company accruing to shareholders. When this "book value" is divided by the number of shares outstanding, one gets a book value per share which is the BV in the P/BV ratio. Say a perusal of a balance sheet results in the finding that

RULE #4. USE COMMON SENSE

They say that one of the most contradictory things about Common Sense is that it isn't! This is especially true when it comes to investing. Not that I can really blame people — every media personality and

UNDERSTANDING FINANCIAL RATIOS (CONTINUED)

a company has total assets of $4 million and total liabilities of $2.5 million. This implies that the shareholders' equity is worth $1.5 million, and if there are 300,000 shares outstanding, then the book value per share is $5. The above company with a share trading at $10 would have a P/BV of 2 (10/5). Of course, the devil is in the details and good investors will comb the statements to reassess the values that are shown in the statements. Sometimes assets like intellectual property do not show up on balance sheets; others, like land, are often undervalued. Still others, like inventories, can be overvalued.

Analysts should look for these and adjust their calculations accordingly. Adjustments may also have to be made for deferred taxes, preferred shares and/or share dilution.

CF is an abbreviation for cash flow. Because earnings of a company can vary significantly from the cash that it generates, and cash generation may be relevant in valuing a company, this ratio is often informative. This value is obtained by looking at the income statement for cash revenue and then only deducting cash expenses. Often a short cut would be to take net income and then add back non-cash expenses such as depreciation, amortization and deferred taxes. If, for example, this calculation amounted to $750,000, and the shares outstanding are 300,000, then cash flow per share is $2.50, and the above company would have a P/CF of 4 (10/2.5). Again, the emphasis is on obtaining a value that is deemed ongoing, realistic, and that can be compared to the value for other companies.

A variable analogous to cash flow that is often quoted and used is EBITDA, which stands for earnings before interest, taxes, depreciation and amortization. EBITDA is of interest in valuing companies in takeover situations because it shows how much cash is generated by the overall company, without regard to its debt or tax situations. This value is less relevant for a private investor who is interested in the company as a going concern.

marketing guru is looking for ways to help us ignore common sense. After all, common sense makes for boring news and dull advertising copy. But ask yourself, why shouldn't we understand the companies we invest in? If you can't figure out how a company makes money, then you shouldn't buy its shares. Look back at Rule #1 – Buy Quality. The quality has to be understandable, defensible and demonstrated over time. Don't overlook the obvious just because it's boring. A good old-fashioned food distribution (grocery store) chain may not seem like an exciting stock, but people have to eat and an established, dominant chain is likely to be the place where they shop. A dominant market share or brand is worth money, but often because it is so familiar and so mundane, eager investors will ignore it. The thinking seems to be, "I can't make money on that stock; everybody knows about it, so it must be fully priced." A fully-priced stock, especially one that pays dividends, can still make you money, but the real benefit comes when the market expects less than what actually ends up happening; in other words, when you Buy Value, if market expectations are low, there is a much better chance that reality will beat expectations.

RULE #5. DON'T OVER-DIVERSIFY

If you own 100 stocks in a portfolio, equally weighted, and one of them doubles in price, your portfolio goes up 1%, all other things being equal. If you own 20 stocks, and one doubles, your portfolio goes up 5%. Diversification is a splendid method for smoothing the ride of a portfolio. It's probably the most widely used shock absorber, but you have to remember that it also dilutes performance. For financial analysts, diversification is intended to eliminate security-specific risk and help a portfolio approximate market risk, but the goal of the Cardinal Rules is to be smoother than the market (see *Understanding Risk and Volatility*, pg. 45).

We don't want to experience the volatility of the market, so we don't buy the market. If you have selected good quality stocks, and

Security risk and market risk, also known as systemic risk, are the yin and yang of risk in the field of investment analysis. Together they are supposed to make up the source of all possible variations in a company's share price. Security risk stems from factors unique to that company or to its industrial sector. This may include input prices, wage levels and labour interruptions, management failings, product demand or any other factor related to the firm and/or its sector that might cause its expected profitability and share price to change. Market risk, on the other hand comes from the other exogenous factors that could cause expected profitability or share price to change. General levels of interest rates, tax rates, economic growth, political uncertainty or international turmoil are such "outside" factors that could change expectations for profit growth or share price fluctuation in a company, but they are not related to any one firm or industry sector and generally impact all or most shares in the market.

Because equities as a whole have demonstrated they can provide higher returns over the long term than other investments, financial analysis and research has largely focused on ways to remove security specific risk, while tolerating market risk. This was done by adding different stocks to a portfolio until the portfolio's behaviour approximated that of the market as a whole. Thus, the security risk from being tied to a specific sector was eliminated, leaving only market risk, and portfolio returns that reflected the premium available from equities as a whole.

waited patiently to buy them at reasonable prices, then why would you diversify away the results of all that hard work? Using the Cardinal Rules should result in a few good solid stock picks. Buy them. Keep them. Let the gradual recognition of their quality by the market show up in the overall value of your portfolio. Besides, it is often difficult to find ten good, reasonably priced stocks, let alone thirty. The data on Cardinal Capital's portfolios indicates that taking this route actually lowers your risk below the market's. (Remember the Risk-Return chart in Chapter 2?) This is achieved because of the quality criteria. The numerical analysis you do on the Balance Sheet and Income Statement weeds out companies with high downside risk, and dividend-paying stocks in general are buffered from the extreme swings that non-dividend paying stocks experience.

Of course, it is possible to take this logic to extremes. A portfolio with one stock in it will double if that stock doubles. But what if after all your analysis, you turn out to be wrong, or an act of God devastates the company you've bought? Some diversification is still prudent, but ten to twenty securities should be adequate in a Cardinal-style portfolio.

A final warning — one danger in buying low is that the market often treats all stocks in one industrial sector alike. Therefore, when you find one cheap bank, for example, you might find several. Make sure you diversify your portfolio by sector as well as by stock. At least three sectors should be represented, although four are better if you can find them. But don't over-diversify; let the value of your picks have some effect.

RULE #6. HOLD WINNERS, SELL LOSERS

If you own a piece of a good company that you bought cheap, and the market finally recognizes the same value that you did so that its market price goes up, why would you sell it? It's still a good company. It's still growing. Remember that the magic of compounding can only have its full effect over time. The old adage in the brokerage industry is "you can't go wrong taking a profit," but this is definitely the wrong attitude for investors. (However, it certainly helps keep trading volume up and, since the old brokerage industry was compensated on a transaction basis, maybe that explains the origin of the saying.) Many investors think they have to lock in profits by selling their winning stocks. But then the cash burns a hole in their pocket and they end up buying a stock that isn't as good as the one they sold!

I've got another great reason not to sell a winning stock. Because then you've got to give the government their share of the profits! When you sell a winning stock, you trigger a capital gain and have to pay the taxes on that gain in that year. If you don't sell the stock, you don't create the gain and you don't pay the tax. You get to use the government's money for as long as you own the stock. For example, say a stock you own is up 10%, bought at $1,000 and worth $1,100. If you sell, you have gains of $100 and must pay capital gains tax on 50% of the value. At a 50% rate, the tax on half the gains ($50) would amount to $25. If you don't sell, the $25 of the $1,100 you have invested is still the government's money, but you get to have the entire $1,100 working for you in your investment. The $25 is money that you would have to pay the government if you sold now, but if you don't sell you can use it to grow your wealth. Let's assume that stock makes 10% in gains in the subsequent year (another $110). If you had paid the government their $25, you would have only had $1,075 invested and would have made only $107.50 in year two. So you made $2.50 using the government's money, of which you would have to pay $0.63 in tax, if you sold it immediately. In other words you made $1.88 on the government's money. The government is not charging you interest – nothing is payable till after you sell it – so you're making a net 7.5% each year on the government's money for which you are paying no interest! That's not a bad return. Compound a 10% return for a few years and you can see that it can turn into real money (See Figure 3-2).

Keep this in mind when you are tempted to sell a winner. You don't have to sell and give the government its money just because events have unfolded as we hoped they would. If you're concerned that it is not a good company anymore, or the market is valuing your company outrageously high, then of course you should consider selling. But don't sell just because the value has gone up. There have to be other reasons to sell.

The tax aspect can influence investors in another way as well. For some investors their reluctance to pay the taxes causes them to

Figure 3-2

Using The Government's Money

Year	Cost	Value	Gain	Tax Owing*	Gain on Tax Owing	Tax Portion* Gov't Money	Gain on Gov't Money	Cum've Gain on Gov't Money
1	$1,000.00	$1,100.00	$100.00	$25.00				
2	1,000.00	1,210.00	210.00	52.50	$2.50	$0.63	$1.88	$1.88
3	1,000.00	1,331.00	331.00	82.75	5.25	1.31	3.94	5.81
4	1,000.00	1,464.10	464.10	116.03	8.28	2.07	6.21	12.02
5	1,000.00	1,610.51	610.51	152.63	11.60	2.90	8.70	20.72
6	1,000.00	1,771.56	771.56	192.89	15.26	3.82	11.45	32.17
7	1,000.00	1,948.72	948.72	237.18	19.29	4.82	14.47	46.63
8	1,000.00	2,143.59	1,143.59	285.90	23.72	5.93	17.79	64.42
9	1,000.00	2,357.95	1,357.95	339.49	28.59	7.15	21.44	85.87
10	1,000.00	2,593.74	1,593.74	398.44	33.95	8.49	25.46	111.33
11	1,000.00	2,853.12	1,853.12	463.28	39.84	9.96	29.88	141.21
12	1,000.00	3,138.43	2,138.43	534.61	46.33	11.58	34.75	175.96
13	1,000.00	3,452.27	2,452.27	613.07	53.46	13.37	40.10	216.05
14	1,000.00	3,797.50	2,797.50	699.37	61.31	15.33	45.98	262.03
15	1,000.00	4,177.25	3,177.25	794.31	69.94	17.48	52.45	314.48

*At 50% capital gains inclusion rate for investor in 50% marginal tax bracket.

hold a stock too long. If you hold the stock for a few years and an initial $1,000 is now worth $2,000, you owe the government $250 when you sell it. Some investors will actually avoid selling just because they don't want to write the cheque to the government. I understand the sentiment, but don't let your feelings about taxes colour your investment decisions. If it's time to sell, it's time to sell. When valuing a portfolio with winners in it, it helps to remember that some of the value belongs to the government. It's not all yours. If you remember that your share of a $100,000 portfolio is only $90,000 it makes it easier to write the $10,000 cheque when the time comes.

Of course, it's also conceivable that after all your analysis and patience, you were wrong in selecting a stock. It may become apparent that there are flaws with the company that you did not appreciate and that the market does. You are now stuck with a loser. Rule #1 – Buy Quality equates to Own or "Hold" Quality. If it's not quality, you don't want to own it. However, it is human nature to try to avoid the loss that will become reality when you sell a loser. The natural inclination is to hold the "dog" until you can get back at least the purchase price. That's a mistake. Cut your losses, sell it, and have the government kick in for their share of your capital loss. (You're getting the picture on this tax thing, right? You owe them – postpone as long as you can. They owe you – collect as soon as you can.)

Hold your winners, sell your losers – with your actions always based on your assessment of quality. Keep the good stocks and sell the bad – based on the facts, not on the market's valuations. Simple to state – hard to execute.

RULE #7. EMPHASIZE LIQUIDITY

Liquidity in a financial context is a measure of an asset's ready convertibility to or from cash. Most shares are fairly liquid, particularly in comparison to "hard" assets like real estate or an automobile. On the stock market you can offer your shares for sale and usually a sale can be executed within a day, with cash received three days later. GICs on the other hand are illiquid, except at maturity; they generally cannot be converted into cash in the interim. However, not all stocks are created equal and liquidity varies with how many you are trying to buy or sell in proportion to how many are usually traded. If a stock trades just a few (or nil) shares in a day, it is said to be thinly traded or illiquid. If the average trading volume in a share (quoted on most financial sites and media) is only 10,000 shares a day and you are trying to buy or sell 20,000 (or even 5,000) it is likely that you will have to wait several days to complete your order and/or that you will have to pay more or sell for less than you would like in order to complete your buy or sell.

When choosing your stocks it is important to remember that flexibility in investing is worth something. When buying or selling stocks you are at the mercy of the market. Luckily, being patient (Rule #3), gives you the opportunity to wait for the market to meet your terms. However, if you choose stocks that are thinly traded, meaning only a few are generally traded in a day, it means that the market's madness is magnified. Opportunities in thinly traded stocks can be few and far between and no amount of patience will suffice if the market in a stock is so thin that the price never comes close to what you have decided (based on your analysis of financial data) is its real value. It follows that illiquid stocks are often perpetual performance laggards. No matter how solid the fundamentals, the share price never seem to reflect reality. As the economist John Maynard Keynes is quoted, "The market can be illogical longer than you can be illiquid."

In this unpredictable world there can be occasions when you desperately need cash in a hurry. Thinly traded stocks don't really have much of a market, meaning selling opportunities may never appear, even for a patient investor. So avoid them. Successful investing is difficult enough without adding the handcuffs of dealing in illiquid securities. Instead you want to emphasize liquidity when choosing your stocks. High volume stocks with large proportions of their shares publicly traded have that liquidity. When thousands of shares trade daily, it is relatively easy for you to get a fill on any order you place.

RULE #8. AVOID MARKET TIMING

The market can be truly irrational. It anticipates what investors are afraid might happen and it reacts to meaningless data in unpredictable ways. Yet many investors believe they can identify when the market is overvalued or when it is undervalued. The constant pundit buzz that the market is over or undervalued can be a major distraction. And the pundits may be right. The market might be over or undervalued at any point in time, but it can stay that way for a long time and no one knows when it will return to its "proper" place. So market timing is nearly impossible, but regardless of that, trying to "time the market" doesn't make any sense for Cardinal-style investors who aren't buying the whole market anyway.

For investors who are only picking low-priced, quality assets, the market's overall level of valuation is irrelevant. What we are interested in is certain individual stock values and the ongoing ownership of quality assets. When we buy we are making an assessment of the market's relative valuation of that one stock, and only that one stock. In a sense we are "market timing" but only that one stock, based on our own assessment of its real value. It makes sense to try and do that on a stock-specific basis. It does not make sense to compound the possibility of timing error by waiting for our specific stock to be cheap at the same time as we believe the overall market is cheap. Waiting for an "overheated market to correct" before we pick our quality stock may actually work against us. Often stock prices for quality stocks move counter to the market. In a market tumble, the so-called "flight to quality" can stabilize or increase the prices of quality stocks. In other instances share prices for underpriced, quality assets may steadily creep higher even as the overall market does nothing. We're not buying the market; just the stock. If it's cheap, buy it.

Once we have bought our stock, we shouldn't really care what the market thinks of it, as long as we are confident in its inherent quality. If it gets cheaper, maybe we can buy more. If it gets more expensive — good. That was our objective. If the whole market gets more expensive, what does it matter? We own the securities we want to own and will likely do better owning them than trading out and back in.

UNDERSTANDING DIVIDEND REINVESTMENT

Some larger, dividend-paying firms have special Dividend Reinvestment Programs (DRIP) that allow their shareholders to have their dividends reinvested in company shares without the expense of going through a stock-broker. Details about these programs are usually available under "Investor Relations" or "Shareholder Information" on the company's website, or by contacting their Investor Relations departments.

RULE #9. REINVEST INCOME

They say that Albert Einstein once declared the eighth wonder of the world to be "compound interest." The magic of compounding turns savers into millionaires. The Cardinal Rules' emphasis on dividend-paying, quality stocks, means that your portfolio will have a steady stream of income to be reinvested. Use it to buy more quality assets either at your discretion or through a Dividend Reinvestment Program (see *Understanding Dividend Reinvestment*, above).

This gets compounding working for you, since each new share purchased will also start paying dividends. That is another reason why dividend payments and a record of dividend growth are so important in identifying quality stocks under Rule #1. If you do not require income from your portfolio, that income can be reinvested and start compounding. Of course, as we become dependent on the portfolio for living income, this may become less possible; however, deferring that income for a few extra years does give your assets that extra chance of building in size before generating income for you.

RULE #10. BUILD WEALTH

Remember the groaning shelves of financial self-help books that I mentioned earlier? Well I expect that each one of them has a chapter about this rule. This is the one our parents tried to teach us at an early age (or should have) and the one that probably makes the most difference in becoming wealthy. Save. Pay Yourself First. A reasonable amount of your income should be regularly salted away into investments. Each week, pay-cheque or month, take a set amount and add it to your investment portfolio. Use it to buy more shares of high quality stocks at reasonable prices. Don't add new stocks, just new shares. (Remember Rule #5 – Don't Over-Diversify.) Resist the temptation to buy the hot stock or to try the new thing. Remember, we're in this for the security, not to win the lottery. We want to be bored with our portfolios.

RULE #11. STAY BALANCED

While this may sound like advice from a psychiatrist, it also works in financial terms. Despite the shock absorbers available for equity investments, it is very calming to also hold the more stable and predictable asset classes. Greed is a terrible thing and it is amazing to see how it can blossom after big successes in equity investing. Early on in this book we talked about how it would be nice to be able to afford not to invest in the stock markets at all, because they can be dangerous. If you had sufficient assets, you could actually stay out of the markets and have a much more relaxed existence as a result. Unfortunately, most of us cannot afford to retire on the minimal growth available from fixed income investments like bonds and GICs. That is why we are learning the Cardinal Rules. But if we get so enamoured with equity markets that we start exposing our nest-eggs to more risk than is warranted, it is sort of like throwing out the baby with the bathwater.

Remember in Chapter 2, Figures 2-5 and 2-8 showed Retirement Planning Charts that assumed constant growth and then showed how fluctuations in price can really mess up the plan. The Cardinal Rules can smooth the ride on your equity portfolio, but it can't eliminate all the risk inherent in equity investment. Your portfolio still needs an element of bonds or GICs, especially if you require income from the portfolio. Equity investments, even with shock absorbers, will fluctuate in value. If you are dependent on your portfolio for living income, it is terrible to have to sell equities when they are at depressed prices in order to get that income. Equities are only close to sure things in the long term. We may not have a long term left, but it is possible to buy some time by protecting a few years of income with fixed and stable investments. In other words, you need to consider how your assets are "allocated" within your portfolio.

The Asset Allocation Advantage

Asset allocation is a term you've likely heard before. It is the cornerstone of modern portfolio management, predicated on the assumption that different classes of securities behave in different ways and that by combining elements of the various classes one can design a portfolio that is likely to have certain behaviourial characteristics. Initially, asset allocation research identified three classes based on the security of returns — cash, bonds and equities. Cash was very secure with low returns, bonds were fairly secure with higher returns, and equities were least secure (most volatile) with the highest long-term returns. Besides return and risk, the research identified one other characteristic of each asset class and that was how the asset classes were correlated. For example, bond and equity returns don't always move in the same way. Sometimes when bond prices fall, equity prices increase, and vice-versa.

Investors can take advantage of this correlation between bonds and equities to get higher returns at lower levels of risk because of the mathematics of correlation. The more differently two asset classes behave, the more advantage there may be in combining them into a single portfolio. This is shown in Figure 3-3, which is a Risk/Return chart. Figure 3-3 shows what would have been the results of investing in different mixes of Canadian bonds and Canadian equities in the twenty years from January 1980 till January 2000. You can see that the safe investment in 100% bonds earned a very low return, but that you could have added as much as 30% equities, thereby increasing returns significantly but not appreciably increasing risk. Sort of a free ride for investors!

Large institutional investors like charitable foundations and pensions have been using this fact in designing their portfolios for a number of years. Consider two pension plans, one that is receiving contributions from a large number of employees and paying out pensions to only a small number of retirees, and another that has only a small number of employees still working and a large number of retirees. (Think Microsoft for the former and General Motors for the latter.) The first pension plan is still growing and has the incoming cash to cushion itself from equity market declines without jeopardizing its payouts. It can take more risk with the equity markets and might allocate its portfolio 40% to bonds and 60% to equities. The second plan, on the other hand, is paying out significantly more each year than it is receiving in contributions. If the value of its portfolio suffers a drop, there is no incoming cash cushion. Its payout obligations to its pensioners may be jeopardized if that occurs. Therefore,

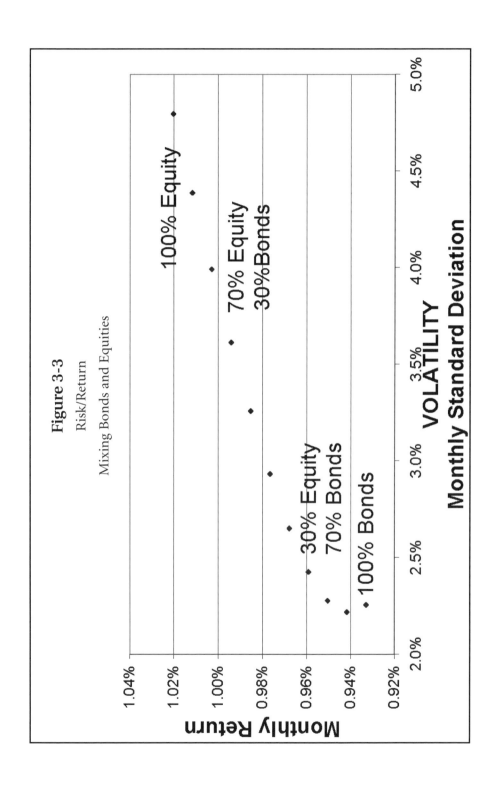

Figure 3-3

Risk/Return

Mixing Bonds and Equities

it is likely to allocate its portfolio far more conservatively, say 20% equities and 80% bonds.

Consequently, as we approach the stage of taking income from our portfolios, it is crucial that we consider safety as well. A certain element of our portfolios should be in safe asset classes like GICs or bonds. One way to do this is to have a ladder of GICs maturing in the amounts that you are going to need for the next few years. This principle is illustrated in Figure 3-4, which shows five years of bonds providing $20,000 per year at a cost of about $90,000 at current yields.

Another alternative might be to invest in a Balanced or Income Fund which would contain bonds or fixed income investments as well as equities. Although boring, it is the prudent route that will avoid potential heartache later.

Subsequent research on asset allocation considered a number of other potential asset classes, including small-capitalization stocks, junk bonds, emerging market equities and emerging market debt, to name a few. Real estate, mortgages, and virtually any group of investments could be deemed a separate asset class for consideration in a portfolio. Unfortunately, several of the smaller or newer asset classes have only a limited historical data set with which to judge their behaviourial characteristics, increasing the risk of adding them to your portfolio. (In most cases these are better left with the professionals and the speculators than with retail investors approaching retirement.)

Another element to be considered in asset allocation decisions is changing circumstances. Historical data from 1980 to 2000 for bonds for instance will show a far higher average return than bonds are likely to show for 2000 to 2020. Interest rates peaked near 20% in 1981 and bonds soared in value as rates fell to the 4% range. We can be pretty sure that interest rates are not going to fall another 16 percentage points in the next few years. Therefore, some economic predictive analysis has to go into estimates about future

Figure 3-4

GIC/Bond Ladder Example

Year	Yield	Income Needed	Face Value to Purchase
1	2.91%	20,000	19,434
2	3.07%	20,000	18,826
3	3.18%	20,000	18,207
4	3.36%	20,000	17,523
5	3.51%	20,000	16,831
		Total	$90,823

behaviours before an asset allocation decision is made.

Most years your equities will outperform your less liquid investments, whether a bond/GIC ladder or an Income/Balanced fund, but never look back at a good year of investing and think, "I should have been all in equities!" Remember we crave boredom. Successful investing is in making what you need to make, not in making as much as possible.

RULE #12. DON'T OVER TRADE

There is an insidious element to investing that causes investors to want to act, rather than watch and wait. Even more insidious is the fact that each investment action (trade) involves direct costs, such as fees and commissions, and indirect costs due to the risk of error. Trading costs are a very real part of any investment management. The more you trade, the higher the costs. The higher the costs, the lower the net return. So the message here is, don't trade unless there is a very compelling reason. Such reasons might include, firstly, a selected quality stock falling to the low price you have set to buy it at; or secondly, an identified quality issue that causes a stock to no longer meet the Buy Quality rule; or thirdly, enough dividends and cash have accumulated to warrant purchasing additional shares of a quality holding. If your trading can be limited to these occasions, your trading costs should remain reasonable.

The indirect costs of trading lie in the risk of error. Investing has often been described as a "Loser's Game." That is, it is like amateur golf or tennis, where the winner is usually the player who makes the fewest mistakes, rather than the player who has the best offense. Every trade executed in a portfolio is an opportunity to make a mistake. The more trades, the higher the likelihood of more mistakes. I love the saying: "An investment portfolio is like a bar of soap. The more you touch it, the smaller it gets!" I recognize that this is a very negative view of potential trades, but history shows that over the long term, quality equities provide a healthy return; frequent interference with this process through trading is more likely to reduce returns than enhance them.

IN A NUTSHELL...

That's it. That's all there is — the Cardinal Rules of Investing made easy. And it's not a secret. As Charlie Munger says about the success he and Warren Buffett have had at Berkshire Hathaway: ". . . success wasn't based on hyper-kinetic activity. It was achieved through a combination of non-diversification, a hell of a lot of patience, and intensely opportunistic behaviour on a few occasions." Warren Buffett adds: "I'd say temperament is still the most important thing ... " And that is probably the most difficult part. One absolutely must leave the emotional baggage behind despite all the pressure around us to knee-jerk react to external events and opinions.

CHAPTER FOUR

Putting the Rules Into Practice

You may think the Cardinal Rules sound too easy, just a bit too cut and dried. While that may be true of the Rules, the execution is often less so. Let's go back over a number of years and look at Cardinal Capital Management's holdings, trades and portfolio activity, so that we can see how the Cardinal Rules were put into practice during the years when Cardinal's amazing track record was being established.

LOOK FOR STABILITY

Back in 1993 at the inception of Cardinal, four quality sectors were identified for investment, including the banking sector, the telephone companies, the pipeline and utility sector, and the integrated oil and gas sector. In each case the large players in the sector had a legal or practical near-monopoly status that reassured investors their earnings would be at least as stable as the market as a whole. Stability is a key element of the Quality that the Cardinal Rules demand. People will always need energy products and financial and telephone services. Huge providers of these services or commodities, with well-recognized brand names, are generally very successful companies. Of course it is possible that new trends and new competitors will negatively impact these companies. But, it is also probable that these companies will identify such new trends and incorporate them into their businesses so as to continue to grow. They generally have the market position to do that. For example, if hydrogen becomes the automotive fuel of choice sometime in the future, I suggest that it is likely that Imperial Oil, Shell Canada and Petrocan, with their extensive and established distribution systems, will be significant players in that market. In the meantime they enjoy near domination of the fuel distribution business. They have a large foothold in the refining of fuel products and have significant reserves of oil and gas, while their exploration and development operations are focused on finding more. Best of all, they are paying healthy dividends to reward investors who hold their stock. As things stand we shouldn't fear for the future of these companies.

What would you consider to be the most boring set of Canadian securities available to buy? Which stocks would you think least likely to hold untapped value because they are closely monitored and widely owned by almost all big investors in Canada? If you're like me, you'd put Canadian bank stocks in that category — boring, already richly priced and not a great buy. That's how I've always thought of them, as securities that are really safe, don't fluctuate much, and therefore only offer a 5% to 6% return potential. Yet the Cardinal Rules point us in the direction of stocks just like these, especially today when dividend yields are fairly high.

Canadian banks are generally highly profitable and have been growing profits fairly steadily for most years of their existence. There are huge political, legal and financial barriers to establishing a new bank in Canada, which reduces overall competition in the sector and allows the banks to act almost as an oligopoly. In general, monopolies and oligopolies have a tremendous ability to protect their profit margins. And, when margins can be preserved, then growth in revenue flows through to growth in profits. In addition to this, the demographics of Canada's aging population means that the overall societal level of savings is increasing, and that increases the business available to the financial sector. This underpins the banks' revenue growth, making for increased profits under protected margins. These factors have been magnified by the development of new technologies which allow the banks to drastically increase the productivity of their employees and, as a result, to cut their costs dramatically. ATMs, for example, can serve clients 24/7 without being paid overtime or needing coffee breaks. This means that not only are profit margins being preserved at reasonable levels, they are actually improving significantly. All of this makes the financial sector an attractive Quality proposition for investors. They have been, and are, a core portion of a portfolio created using the Cardinal Rules.

Take a look at the shares of Canada's biggest bank, the Royal Bank of Canada (RBC). In May of 1993 shares of RBC were priced at $28.50 and had an annual dividend rate of $0.58 per share or a yield of 2.04% (0.58/28.50). RBC was a huge conservative company with an established dividend in a mature industry and market. It had experienced a loss in 1992 and a much reduced profit in 1993 after several excellent years at the end of the 1980s. Despite the loss in 1992 and the low profit in 1993, the bank had preserved its dividend rate. (Remember management is extremely hesitant to reduce a dividend rate once it is established.) In 1993, the five-year dividend payout was 72%, meaning that of the annual average net income per share earned by the bank over the years 1989 through 1993, 72% was paid out in annual dividends. This is a relatively high proportion, but not dangerously so, especially when one remembers that the bank had just weathered a couple of bad years. The analysis of all these factors led Tim Burt to add Royal Bank stocks to his clients' portfolios at Cardinal Capital.

This stock actually did very well for shareholders over the

next twelve years. As of May 31, 2005, a share was worth $75, for an appreciation of over 260%. But this tells only a small part of the story, because in October of 2000, every shareholder of RBC was issued another share at no charge. Therefore for your investment of $28.50 in one share in 1993, you now had an investment of two shares worth $75 each or $150, for a gain of 526%. This represents a return of 14.8% per year for the twelve years. That's not too shabby for what most would have considered one of the safest stocks you could have chosen in 1993. In fact, the index over that time gained only about 12% per year.

But wait! There's more. Remember that 58-cent dividend? Fifty-eight cents doesn't seem like a big deal, and in isolation it isn't. But there were miraculous things happening through the years following 1993. Profits started to recover nicely in 1994, so that the 72% dividend payout ratio fell to nearer 30%. That 58-cent annual dividend rate went up dramatically as the bank's profits grew. By May 2005, the annual dividend rate at RBC was $2.20 per share, and they had just announced an increase in the August dividend to an annual rate of $2.44 per share. If we had bought our shares at $28.50 in 1993, we'd be collecting $4.88 per share each year because we got those free extra shares in 2000. We would now be earning over 17% per year on our original investment. With yields like that who cares what 5-year GICs are paying?

And still that is not the whole story! What if we had taken the dividend that was paid out every three months and used it to buy more shares? In 1993 each dividend would have bought 0.5% of a share so that the final two dividends, August and November would have resulted in buys of about 1% of a share. Again, this seems like no big deal. But over time using the dividend to buy new shares adds up. By the autumn of 2000 we would have received enough dividends to buy over 13% more shares. If we bought 100 in 1993, we'd have 113 shares in the fall of 2000. Of course that's when we got the free share for every one owned, and suddenly we've got 226 shares instead of just 100. See how the dividend reinvestment helps? In just over seven years our $28.50 has grown to about $108. What about the five years since then? Because of the compounding that occurs, our 226 shares turn into just over 258 shares, and the share price of about $48 goes up to the $75 that we see today. (For a deeper look at the Royal Bank data, see Appendix II.) Our original $28.50 investment has turned into almost $194 for a total appreciation of 679% or an annual compound return of over 17.3%! How come everybody isn't doing this?

Just to emphasize the power of the Cardinal Rules, you should consider that the return on this one stock, terrific as it is at over 17% a year for twelve years, is generally the average Cardinal return over the period! Even with the protection of more diversification than investing in a single stock, the Cardinal portfolios made about 17% per year.

Makes you want to run out and buy bank stocks, doesn't it? But before you write the cheque, you might want to consider this. Canadian bank stocks have had a splendid run as a number of fortuitous and deliberate measures have coincided. Tim still sees Canadian Schedule A banking as a license to print money, but are those shares too expensive now? Remember, of course, the Cardinal Rules do recommend some diversification, especially between sectors. Your total wealth should not be totally exposed to single entity risk, nor even to single sector risk, no matter how carefully it's selected. Remember, we income seekers should value safety and security more highly than return.

BUY AND HOLD? NOT NECESSARILY

How did the other sectors in Cardinal's 1993 portfolios fare? Two of the original core Cardinal sectors have now been demoted, and this points out the need for vigilance and creativity in assessing Quality. "Buy and Hold" is often touted as an investing rule for the conservative investor, and on the surface it seems to make a lot of sense. Buy and Hold assumes that if you "buy" quality, it will always pay off in the long run; hence, you should continue to "hold" your buys. It assumes that the world never changes – or that all change affects all companies equally, which is not necessarily so. Surprisingly perhaps, "buy and hold" is not the practice of the Cardinal Rules. A subtle but important distinction in the Cardinal Rules criteria is to Buy Quality and Hold Quality! This means that stocks should constantly be reviewed and re-assessed to ensure they meet the Quality criterion. Pipelines and utilities are generally now gone from the Cardinal portfolios for reasons of Quality. Many of the pipeline companies have been acquired or merged into larger entities. One remaining independent is TransCanada Pipelines, but even this dividend-paying entity is no longer in the Cardinal portfolio. The Cardinal story about TransCanada is an excellent lesson in the practical application of the Cardinal Rules.

The Cardinal Rules led to the purchase of TransCanada early on. The stock had a consistent dividend (which was showing some growth) and the company had reasonable financial strength. TransCanada stock enjoyed a valuable, stabilizing position in the portfolio for several years. However, in 1998 TransCanada Pipelines started to exhibit symptoms that triggered concern at Cardinal. The 1998 earnings slipped in relation to those of 1997. The balance sheet showed considerably more debt as the company diversified through acquisition in the mid-1990s, taking on extra debt in the process. Tim saw the writing on the wall. Perhaps the post-mortem mea culpa published in the Chairman's Message to Shareholders in the 1999 Annual Report of TransCanada Pipelines puts it most succinctly: TransCanada "made large investments in midstream and in international assets in anticipation of earning substantially higher returns than those in the regulated North American pipeline businesses. . . . In fact . . . the actual earnings from these combined assets in 1999 were negligible and the projected future earnings were diminished." In other words, they made investments to change the company beyond being a pipeline utility, and the results stunk. Tim Burt's regular review of the public financial information from the company through 1998 foresaw this potential outcome. In his opinion the company had lost its Quality character because of the more risky financial structure and suspect dividend yield.

By December 1998, Tim was getting Kelly Berg, his administrative assistant (and now Vice-President of Cardinal) to provide him a list of all clients who owned TransCanada in their portfolios. By June of 1999 all shares of TransCanada had been sold out of Cardinal client accounts. On December 8th of that year, to the dismay and shock of the financial media, TransCanada cut its dividend 29% (from $1.12 per year to $0.80 per year). It's share price fell to close at $11.70 on December 14th, almost half of the $20 plus that it had traded at in July when Tim was divesting Cardinal client shares. By this one action, Tim saved Cardinal clients considerable value. One might argue that the position should never have been purchased initially, but clients benefited from a decent dividend yield and quite stable share price during the period it was owned in their portfolios. It was an ideal holding for an investor living off income from an equity portfolio. (As a footnote: the cover of the TransCanada Pipelines 2000 Annual Report highlighted the company's credo: "Objective: restore and strengthen our financial position.")

Analyse, Analyse, and Re-Analyse

To me, this episode alone speaks to the wisdom of using the Cardinal Rules, but it also points out a major drawback. The strategy does involve work and it does require systematic diligence. Those like me who are only systematic some of the time would have a few problems executing properly. Actions like this make the fees paid to a professional advisor look like great value.

The telephone companies too have been cut from Cardinal's portfolios. In Tim's opinion, the larger, traditional telecom companies seem bent on banging their collective heads against new technologies. They have had a chance to build up scale in their existing markets through acquisitions, but the only meaningful merger in Canada has been Alberta Government Telephones (Telus) and BC Tel. The old telephone majors do still have dominant market positions and established dividend policies — the reasons they were considered Quality buys for the Cardinal portfolios of the past. However, new competitors are generally beating them in the new technology fields and appear to now be in a position to come into traditional local telephone markets. The old companies appear to have squandered their opportunity to become super-competitive and to lock up market share. Across the board profit margins are generally being compressed, which puts dividend growth and even existing dividend levels in jeopardy. They may weather the rough spots over time, but for Tim they no longer meet the Buy Quality criteria.

One might argue that this conclusion seems to belie the argument I made above in regard to the large integrated oil companies and their being able to adapt and profit from future changes. "We shouldn't fear for the future of these companies," I stated, but neither should we use these conditions to justify blind optimism concerning their Quality. Don't fear for the future until the facts warrant the worry, but check the facts!

This is not to say that Tim Burt is infallible in his assessment of quality, nor will you be if you start implementing the Cardinal Rules in your own portfolio. Tim has bought and then sold some companies out of the portfolios because of Quality concerns, only to see the companies struggle through, "revitalize" and achieve new levels of profitability and Quality. Tim has then bought back in at higher prices than he sold at.

You should be warned that for a novice investor, such a trade would be very difficult emotionally. Only someone with experience in the markets knows how painful it can be to lose faith in a stock that you once believed in, and sell it, only to later admit error and face buying it back at a higher price. We humans are generally reluctant to confront our mistakes, so we tend to stall in selling a share dropping in value and delay buying it back when the price is high, hoping that its price will come down to near where we sold it. Difficult as it is, you must try to erase trading history from your mind and evaluate each decision on its own merits. Is the current price now a good one for the Quality and profit/dividend expectations that we have for the company? If so, we should buy, regardless of the past trades we have made in the stock. Professionalism in managing investments takes this kind of fortitude.

Going back to the history of the Cardinal portfolios, the removal of the pipelines and the telecoms in the portfolio meant replacements were needed. To some extent a significant expansion of the financial sector has occurred. World-class insurance companies have de-mutualized and are now publicly traded, and publicly-traded mutual fund companies have some respectable yields and growth rates. The gamut of newer "opportunities" also includes railways and retailers that were not available or were less mature back in 1993-1994. While not necessarily core-sector, the picks still have the market dominance, dividend policy and/or growth rates that comply with the Cardinal Rules.

Figure 4-1 provides a list of securities that were selected for Cardinal portfolios in 1993/1994 using the Cardinal Rules. There are a surprising number of them, thirty in all, but perhaps even more surprising is that eleven of them are no longer traded, having been taken over or merged into other entities. This supports my contention that the Cardinal Rules do identify desirable companies, companies whose quality makes them highly attractive businesses for merger and acquisition. Other business managers appear to have agreed.

You should note that all the stocks on this list did pay a dividend in 1993 and all were profitable. Some non-core sector holdings

Figure 4-1

Canadian Securities Selected (1993-1994) Using the Cardinal Rules*

Name	Price (Dec 31/93)	P/E	Dividend	Dividend Yield
Alberta Energy Company	$18.50	23.7	$0.35	1.9%
Alberta Natural Gas	16.50	14.2	0.68	4.1
Bank of Montreal	27.63	10.7	1.12	4.1
Bank of Nova Scotia	30.63	10.3	1.12	3.7
BC Gas Inc.	16.63	13.0	0.50	5.4
BC Telecom Inc.	25.13	13.4	1.20	4.7
BCE Inc.	46.25	49.2	2.68	5.8
Bruncor Inc.	24.13	13.9	1.28	5.3
Canadian Imperial Bank of Commerce	33.00	11.0	1.32	4.0
Canadian Utilities Class A	25.63	12.3	1.42	5.5
George Weston Ltd.	39.00	25.5	0.70	1.8
Imasco Ltd.	40.13	12.9	1.48	3.7
Imperial Oil Ltd.	44.25	31.3	1.80	4.1
Loblaw Companies Ltd.	22.88	21.0	0.24	1.1
Maple Leaf Foods Inc.	12.88	15.9	0.38	3.0
Nowsco Well Services	19.00	13.8	0.26	1.4
Pacific Northern Gas	22.00	12.8	0.88	4.0
Petro Canada	12.00	19.0	0.13	1.1
Royal Bank of Canada	28.88	62.8	1.16	4.0
Shell Canada Ltd.	38.38	40.8	0.90	2.3
Slocan Forest Products	33.13	14.0	0.24	0.7
TD Bank Financial Group	21.38	26.1	0.76	3.6
Telus Corp.	16.00	13.6	0.92	5.8
Torstar Corp Cl B	24.00	14.0	0.84	3.5
TransAlta Corp.	15.25	13.6	0.98	6.4
TransCanada Pipelines	20.13	12.5	0.92	4.6
Trans-Mountain Pipe	19.50	10.0	0.96	4.9
Weldwood of Canada	24.50	24.7	0.20	0.8
West Fraser Timber	48.00	23.4	0.40	0.8
Westcoast Energy Inc.	22.00	12.3	0.88	4.0
Average		19.7		3.5

* Source: The Globe and Mail, Report on Business; January 1, 1994; pp. B8-9. Corporate Annual Reports.

like Loblaw had great Quality attributes as well as a respectable dividend growth record. What is perhaps unexpected is the presence of names like Slocan, Nowsco, Torstar, Maple Leaf, Weldwood and West Fraser Timber. They did not fit into the near-monopoly, protected status of the other Cardinal sectors selected. Maple Leaf, however, had a sizable market share and brand image; Torstar had a very respectable yield and reasonable dividend growth rate; and Slocan had a relatively low P/E compared to Weldwood and West Fraser. The three forestry companies had lower dividend yields, at less than 1%, and they were not as compelling Quality stories as we would have expected.

The interests in the three forestry companies were closed through 1995, and generally performed well, with Slocan and Weldwood being quite profitable positions and West Fraser being closed with a small loss. Maple Leaf Foods was bought in May 1994 with a significant market share, dominating brands, a modest P/E (16) and relatively decent dividend yield (3%) triggering the purchase at $12.75, which position was closed in March 1995 at $14.75 after the receipt of four dividends. Nowsco had a relatively low P/E of near 14 compared to many in the energy sector which had ratios up near 40. The position was sold in September of 1995 and the quality of the firm was confirmed when it was bought by American oil services giant BJ Services in June of 1996.

The Torstar story is also one of modest quality, but good dividend yield. Bought in late 1994 at 24-3/8, with a P/E of about 14 and dividend yield of 3.5%, the company paid its 21-cent quarterly dividend from Q4-1994 through Q1-1996 when the dividend was increased to 23 cents. The share price moved up to $34 by December 1996 when the shares were divested. Gross return – about 40%.

Tim tells me that some of these early ventures by Cardinal would not pass muster now. The Rules were still being developed in those early days and Tim did not have as much emphasis on dividend yield and growth as is now apparent. In those days Tim paid more attention to the individual company's quality than to the quality that prevails for the sector overall, whereas now, sector quality is an equally important element in stock identification. Nowadays Cardinal shies away from single resource extraction companies, fearing for the volatility caused by commodity prices. Avoiding volatility is Cardinal's "prime directive."

So what about nowadays? Let's look at what would pass the Buy Quality test in today's markets.

Building A Cardinal Portfolio Today

Okay – so the last twelve years have been very good for portfolios using the Cardinal Rules. Great, but now it's 2005, not 1993. Y2K is over, oil is king and interest rates are rising. What would Tim Burt be buying right now? Where would the Cardinal Rules lead him in terms of finding value in today's market?

Because investment decisions depend on individual situations and requirements, I can't make recommendations about specific securities that a reader should purchase for his or her portfolio. However, in this chapter I will review and assess the current market position of a number of individual securities to help you to understand and use the Cardinal Rules' selection criteria. This is not to be considered a recommendation for any reader to buy or sell any particular security. Furthermore, I have tabulated various financial data on a number of companies here. This data was obtained from corporate reports and investment data services and is believed to be accurate; however, there are no assurances. Regardless, the data here is insufficient in and of itself to be used for making investment decisions. It is intended to help show how the Cardinal Rules could be used to assess and compare different companies. Before making any investment decision, individual investors should see a professional advisor, or at least should access the annual reports, financial statements and annual information forms as well as other corporate filings with Canadian and other market regulators. These are available at no charge on corporate websites and at www.sedar.com. If you are considering implementing the Cardinal Rules personally, I strongly recommend that you become familiar with this data, practice using it, and learn to understand it before making any investment decisions.

To assess the application of the Cardinal Rules in today's market universe of stocks, it makes sense to start by looking at what is in the Cardinal portfolios right now. We will also look at a couple of other prospective stocks that are worth considering because of their dividend yield and sector. On that basis I've prepared a list of twenty-three stocks. At the end of this chapter I have included a number of tables showing relevant data such as dividend history(Figure 5-1), earnings per share history (Figure 5-2), and TSE closing prices for the last three years (Figure 5-3) for the group of twenty-three companies. These tables were used to derive three more tables showing dividend payout ratio (Figure 5-4), dividend yield (Figure 5-5) and price/earnings (trailing) ratios (Figure 5-6).

In this group of twenty-three companies there are twenty that are currently in most of the Cardinal Canadian equity portfolios. These include the big five chartered banks, the three integrated oil companies, three insurance companies, the two Canadian railways, two mutual fund companies, one auto-parts manufacturer, one food producer, one grocery chain and two that are mining-resource oriented. These firms are all in the Cardinal portfolios right now. In addition I've added two pipeline utilities (TransCanada Pipeline and Atco) and an electrical utility (TransAlta) to allow even more comparison.

All of the 23 companies are paying a dividend, and all are currently profitable. There has been growth in most of the dividends since 2004 as shown in Figure 5-1, and, as one would expect from a period when the economy is recovering from a slowdown such as we saw in 2001, generally a growth in profits as seen in the earnings per share in Figure 5-2. Note that one exception is TransAlta whose dividend is flat and whose earnings are actually going down. A few of the companies have had a loss in the last five years, but that appears to have been a mainly temporary or extraordinary event rather than a trend. For some, earnings growth has been exponential. CI Funds, for instance has gone from a profit of 6 cents a share in 2001 to a profit of $0.82 per share in 2004 (Figure 5-2). For the group of 23 in general, the average growth per year in earnings per share is over 14%. Remember this is not a group of high-growth, small and nimble technology companies. This list is the crème de la crème of big Canadian blue-chip corporations. Growth of 14% per year is not something most would have anticipated for this group, especially with the base year of 2000 being pretty much the last year of a boom. Maybe such growth can continue, but possibly not.

In talking to Tim about his track record, he indicated that in the current environment he would be focusing his search for acceptable stocks primarily on companies that are experiencing dividend growth of 5% or more. You can see that almost all of the companies currently in his portfolio qualify under this criterion with only five companies in the Tables (including TransAlta) not achieving 5% growth, and with an average dividend growth for the entire group at over 10% (Figure 5-1). Whether this growth can continue or not depends in large part on how earnings continue to grow, but dividend payout ratios do tell us whether companies are coming close to bumping their heads on cash limits.

If we look at the dividend payouts we may get some inkling about prospective growth. But note that as earnings fluctuate, the payout ratio swings, sometimes to extremes. Looking at a five-year history, such as in Figure 5-4, helps put the annual data in perspective. However, this does not mean that the short-term swings should be ignored. Instead when analyzing this data you should look for the anomalies — the sharp rises and falls or interruptions in patterns — and research why these may have occurred. Remember that we stated in Chapter 3 that a portion of profits retained by the company is often reinvested for growth. If so, we would hope that if a company is retaining a good portion of profits, then future growth can be expected to be quite healthy. On this measure, TransAlta again appears to be falling short. It has paid out an average of 80% of its profits over the last five years (Figure 5-4), yet its earnings continue to decline (Figure 5-2). Can it continue to maintain its dividend? While the answer lies only in the future, a look at the company's balance sheet and cash flow would provide some clues. In particular, you could look at how much of a cash cushion is available, how substantial are retained earnings, and how much cash is being used up for capital expansion or maintenance and replacement.

On average the Dividend Payout Ratio for the group is pretty good at about 36%, indicating that most firms are probably retaining enough of their profits to maintain healthy growth. TransCanada Pipelines is paying out an average of 60%, although in the last year the ratio improved to 54%. TD Financial had a one year loss in 2002 which raises its average payout. And CI Funds appears to be paying out dividends in anticipation of high growth in earnings so that its current payout ratio is quite high. The insurance companies and the railways are paying out only about 20%, indicating that future growth (or future dividend growth) is quite likely. PetroCanada has a very low payout (even compared to its industry peers) coupled with quite good earnings history. Is this a sign that dividend increases are likely? Again, look to the balance sheets to see the cash or short-term assets position. Imperial Oil has a tendency to maintain relatively low dividend payouts, but pay out special dividends when what might be called "windfall" profits accumulate from high oil prices. Is PetroCanada taking this route? Is Imperial Oil due for another special dividend?

Figure 5-3 shows the share prices at the fiscal year ends for the last three years, and when these are coupled with the eps data shown in Figure 5-2, you will get the trailing P/E ratios for each of those years (Figure 5-6). The average of the P/E ratios for 2004 is just over 15, whereas the P/E for the TSX as a whole as of July 2005 was about 19. This demonstrates that the Buy Value criteria is being met by holding these companies, which are generally cheaper than the market index, and cheaper than they were over the last two years. Given that profit growth is expected to continue for these companies, it means that the prospective P/E ratio is even lower than 15. However, it is notable that PetroCanada and Atco have P/E ratios meaningfully lower than the average.

Figure 5-6 also shows the volatility of P/E ratios for some companies. Look at TD Financial whose multiple has gone from –117 to 14 in just three years, or Imperial Oil which dropped from 99 in 2003 to 12 in 2004. This demonstrates the need to "normalize" earnings per share to account for year-to-year variations as a method of estimating earnings going forward. This can involve complicated financial modeling of each company, but a simpler, conservative approach would be to rely on history. Figure 5-7 shows normalized earnings per share for the group derived by simply calculating the average eps over a longer period, such as the five years shown in Figure 5-2, then using this number to calculate a normalized P/E at the end of fiscal 2004.

Note that this approach works better with companies that are mature and whose earnings are on a reasonably stable track. For companies with a strong up or down trend in earnings, such as CI Funds, the result is less useful. In this instance, projecting earnings at a growth rate conservatively based on history is likely to be more informative.

From Figure 5-7 you can see that PetroCanada, at a normalized P/E of 13.2, is trading at a lower average than its peer group. Other companies, Loblaw as an example, appear a little richly priced by comparison. TransCanada Pipelines is trading at a higher ratio than the other utility-type companies, and considering all the measurements for the prospect companies, of the three it appears that only Atco might qualify under the Cardinal Rules.

Lastly, we can use the data in the tables to calculate Dividend Yield as shown in Figure 5-5. While yields are not as rich as two years ago, almost all of these companies are paying out at a rate higher than bank accounts or money market funds. At least some return is being made to the shareholders by management as a reward for holding the stock. As previously noted, this yield acts as a stabilizer on the share price (giving us some of the safety that we are looking for) as well as reassuring us about management's expectations for earnings going forward.

SECTOR CONSIDERATION

Each of the sectors in this group has a Quality story to tell, and each of the companies chosen for the Cardinal Capital portfolios shows a solid business model for continuing its success. As he did in 1993 (and virtually continuously since then) Tim still sees the banks and insurance companies as a core sector with excellent long-term prospects. As previously mentioned, demographic and technological trends favour them and the legal and regulatory environment provide them some cushion from cut-throat competition. Their dividend policy and balance sheet information fit solidly into the Buy Quality category.

The integrated oils are another key sector. Note that the integrated companies, such as Imperial Oil, Shell Canada and PetroCanada, differ from most energy stocks in that their revenue and profitability is not solely dependent on the price of oil, but is also derived from the refining and distribution of oil products. In retail markets the three majors each have a commanding market share and solid brand recognition. Therefore the impact of oil price swings on their exploration and reserves is buffered by the stability and profitability of their other activities.

The railways (CNR and CPR) have a dominant market position with revenues dependent on overall economic activity and they are still benefiting from technology changes. Unlike many industries, the railways stand to benefit from the Asian boom as they are paid to ship raw materials to seaports and to bring back foreign goods from those ports.

The mutual fund industry and insurance industry both benefit from the same demographics as favour the banks and from the same technological trends. Economies of scale in these industries can be massive and larger companies are quite profitable. The insurance companies also have opportunities to expand in foreign markets.

In the resource/mining sector, Finning International and Teck-Cominco both stand to benefit from the boom in resource prices. Finning is a more strategic call since its right to distribute Caterpillar equipment to the mining sector gives it brand image clout that is not usually available in the commoditized resource business.

The remaining holdings, Loblaw, Magna and Saputo, are less strategic and more tactical. They add more sectors to the mix for diversification, and they are quality companies with strong market positions in understandable industries.

One might question why an auto parts manufacturer such as Magna International warrants the quality assessment to be on this list, particularly when one understands the extent of automobile production over-capacity in the developed world and the weakened financial state of many of the traditional automobile producers. Tim's belief is that companies such as Magna will benefit significantly from the inevitable future rationalization in the automotive sector. Companies that in the past have produced many of their own parts and vehicles will outsource much of the metal-bashing, metal-cutting, plastic molding activities of production, and possibly even most assembly operations, with a possible end result being that the car companies themselves will come to focus mainly on design and marketing. Companies like Magna may realize economies of scale by producing cars for many car companies. The biggest drawback Tim sees in Magna is its multi-class share ownership structure, which structure it shares with a number of Canadian companies. Subordinated voting shares are what are widely available to public investors such as us, while the majority of votes rest with another, less available, share class. The Quality criterion would indicate that each shareholder should be able to vote in proportion to his or her investment, but this is not the case here. The counter-argument to this is that the controlling shareholder (often the founder), is so heavily involved and committed to the organization that only he can truly know how best to run the firm. This of course also raises the possibility of significant conflicts between the interests of the shareholder/manager and the subordinated investors. In the case of Frank Stronach, for example, who controls Magna, there have been a number of widely-publicized disagreements between himself and other shareholders about his compensation and his strategy for the company. Is this enough to disqualify Magna from a Cardinal holding? In Tim's eyes, the risk is very real, but insufficient to disqualify it. However, the risk must be continually monitored — another reason why you may consider professional, full-time money management essential. Alternatively, if you don't have the time or skill to monitor situations such as this, this type of ownership structure alone might be considered sufficient to disqualify a company from your portfolio.

Several of the companies on this list may not have perpetual positions in the portfolio and might be traded out as values or fundamentals change. The grocery chain, Sobey's, for example, was until recently in Cardinal portfolios. When the U.S. grocery chain A&P announced that they were selling off their Canadian assets, located primarily in the Ontario market, Sobey's expressed their intent to bid for the assets. Tim felt that, given the state of their balance sheet, an acquisition of the A&P assets at a reasonable value would probably make the firm's financial structure too risky for his comfort (the debt-equity ratio would become too high). On the other hand, if Sobey's was unsuccessful and a competitor bought the A&P assets, the bigger, stronger competition from the combined assets would affect Sobey's growth and profitability, particularly in the Canadian market's "sweet-spot" of southern Ontario. Sobey's would be negatively affected either way. Consequently, Sobey's was sold out of Cardinal's portfolios. Its Quality attribute was lost.

A newer entrant on the Canadian stock pages is the Income or Royalty Trust. These entities often have a much higher dividend yield and are mature businesses compared to other stocks. However, these attributes alone do not qualify such trusts as Cardinal Rules' picks nor does their trust nature disqualify them. Each entity must be considered on its own merits and that of its sector, using the same type of analysis and strategic assessment you would use for any company, with Quality being the key consideration. With many trusts the business model and the financial structure are the major concern. In general, trusts are not expected to grow substantively in the future. That is why they pay out most of their income as dividends instead of re-investing it. Many royalty trusts have a limited asset base with which to work. It can be a depleting asset, which means that at some point in the future (when the asset base is used up), the dividends will end and the shares (units) may then well be worthless. Is the stream of dividends rich enough and does it have enough longevity to warrant the erosion of capital? Some business trusts, such as Gaz Metro and Inter Pipeline Fund are basically utilities. Safe and high-yielding, this type of trust is worth considering under the Cardinal Rules.

It is not a Cardinal sin to want to have a Quality, high-yielding, no-growth business in your portfolio if it has some longevity, but don't be seduced by the high yield. Such a stock can add safety to your portfolio, even if it may be limited in its upside return, but carefully consider how big or how small a portion of the overall portfolio you want such trust units to comprise.

Real estate investment trusts (REITs), on the other hand, generally yield well and have a value related to the real estate market, which you should note differs in behaviour from that of the stock market. (Remember our discussion of correlation in Asset Allocation in Chapter 3?) Some real estate in a portfolio complements equities quite well, although many Canadians, particularly our age, already have real estate in the form of their home and/or second residence. Remember, diversification applies here as well, and it is prudent not to become too exposed to any one asset class, including real estate, especially when it appears that prices may be reaching unsustainable levels.

I hope this presentation and comparison of data for specific companies has given you a taste of what's involved in using the Cardinal Rules to select and manage the stocks in your portfolio at mid-2005. As times change different companies see different prospects and are priced differently by the market. Still, these are equities and there is always the possibility that unforeseen and unforeseeable events will destroy part of their value in spite of all the precautions that have been taken in selecting them. However, the Cardinal approach of maintaining a mix of 20 quality stocks, across a variety of sectors and companies, means that even if one or two of these stocks implodes, then the others should provide enough growth to protect the portfolio value.

Of particular note is that the logic behind the analysis of Magna and Sobey's (and the telephone companies discussed in Chapter 4) illustrates an important element in the successful management of an investment portfolio. The decisions concerning these companies do not depend on complex mathematical analysis. Nor do they depend on arcane financial data that can only be gleaned by a team of whiz-kids in green eyeshades. Rather, these cases demonstrate the need to think strategically and to think outside the box, as the cliché goes. Remember, ignore the headlines and think and act strategically. What external trends and factors exist, and how will they affect the companies? Which good companies are well situated to help them prosper in their markets over the next few years? Therein lie the potential candidates for the Cardinal Rules. The universe in five years is unlikely to be the same as it is now, but I would bet, based on history, that the stocks Cardinal owns now, will have provided a decent return over that time. Broad, creative approaches to an industry's future and a company's role in that future come from a varied, well-rounded background and world view coupled with serious unbiased logic. A chess-player or history buff may well make a better investment manager than an MBA, just because of the strategic focus that both have.

This is where Tim Burt seems to excel. The combination of his risk-aversion, his concern for protecting client wealth and his strategic foresight, help him identify and act on signs and situations such as the TransCanada Pipeline dividend cut of 1999. He may well be wrong in future. The telephone companies may go on to reap extraordinary profits and grow like gangbusters. If so, Tim has erred in his read of their future. But the error is based on a logical, strategic view of the future.

So how did Tim develop this strategic insight? To understand some of what makes Tim tick, it would perhaps help to look at his career and his progression from U.S. equity analyst and U.S. portfolio manager to independent Canadian equity manager and entrepreneur. Reviewing the education and experience of Tim Burt in the investment management industry should show us some of the factors that helped develop and refine the Cardinal Rules.

Figure 5-1

Cardinal Rules

Potential Stock Picks for 2005

Dividend Paid by Fiscal Year

	2004	2003	2002	2001	2000	Growth
Banks						
CIBC	$2.20	$1.64	$1.60	$1.44	$1.29	11.3%
TD Financial	1.36	1.16	1.12	1.09	0.92	8.1
Bank of Montreal	1.50	1.29	1.18	1.09	0.99	8.7
Royal Bank of Canada	2.02	1.72	1.52	1.38	1.14	12.1
Bank of Nova Scotia	1.10	0.84	0.73	0.62	0.50	17.1
Insurance						
Sun Life	0.86	0.68	0.56	0.48		15.7
Manulife	0.94	0.78	0.60	0.48	0.30	25.7
Great West Lifeco	0.69	0.56	0.47	0.39	0.33	16.1
Mutual Fund Companies						
CI Funds	0.41	0.29	0.06	0.05	0.05	52.0
Investors Group	1.15	0.99	0.86	0.73	0.61	13.5
Integrated Oils						
Imperial Oil	0.88	0.87	0.84	0.83	0.78	2.4
PetroCanada	0.60	0.40	0.40	0.40	0.40	8.5
Shell Canada	0.94	0.82	0.80	0.80	0.76	4.3
Railroads						
CNR	0.78	0.67	0.57			10.9
CPR	0.52	0.51	0.51			0.7
Resource/Mining						
Finning	0.40	0.36	0.30	0.20	0.20	14.9
Teck-Cominco	0.30	0.20	0.20	0.20	0.20	8.5
Miscellaneous						
Loblaw	0.76	0.60	0.48	0.40	0.40	13.7
Magna International (US)	1.48	1.36	1.36	1.36	1.24	3.6
Saputo	0.60	0.48	0.40			14.5
Prospects						
TransCanada Pipelines	1.17	1.08	1.00	0.90	0.80	7.9
Atco	1.40	1.20	1.16	1.04	0.92	8.8
TransAlta	1.00	1.00	1.00	1.00	1.00	0.0
Average						10.5

Figure 5-2

Cardinal Rules

Potential Stock Picks for 2005

EPS by Fiscal Year

	2004	2003	2002	2001	2000	Grth
Banks						
CIBC	$5.53	$5.18	$1.35	$4.13	$4.90	2.5%
TD Financial	3.39	1.51	-0.25	2.05	1.53	17.3
Bank of Montreal	4.42	3.44	2.68	2.66	3.25	6.3
Royal Bank of Canada	4.23	4.39	3.93	3.52	3.51	3.8
Bank of Nova Scotia	2.82	2.34	1.65	2.02	1.81	9.3
Insurance						
Sun Life	2.79	2.15	1.83	2.07	1.48	13.5
Manulife	3.62	3.31	2.88	2.38	2.22	10.3
Great West Lifeco	1.78	1.46	1.25	0.70	0.86	15.7
Mutual Fund Companies						
CI Funds	0.82	0.31	-0.35	0.06		92.3
Investors Group	2.24	2.03	1.85	1.05	1.35	10.7
Integrated Oils						
Imperial Oil	5.74	0.58	3.20	3.11	3.37	11.2
PetroCanada	6.55	6.16	3.59	3.67	3.16	15.7
Shell Canada	4.64	2.92	2.02	3.65	3.04	8.8
Railroads						
CNR	4.34	3.49	2.65			17.9
CPR	2.60	2.52	3.06	2.34	3.17	-3.9
Resource/Mining						
Finning	1.43	1.68	1.69	1.34	0.94	8.8
Teck-Cominco	2.99	0.68	0.06	-0.17	0.66	35.3
Miscellaneous						
Loblaw	3.51	3.05	2.62	2.04	1.71	15.5
Magna International (US)	7.13	5.19	5.79	6.20	6.44	2.1
Saputo	2.20	2.03	1.54	1.07	0.99	17.3
Prospects						
TransCanada Pipelines	2.14	1.77	1.55	1.30	1.45	8.1
Atco	5.35	4.39	5.48	4.17	3.78	7.2
TransAlta	0.88	1.26	1.17	1.27	1.66	-11.9
Average						14.1

Figure 5-3

Cardinal Rules

Potential Stock Picks for 2005

Share Price Close at Fiscal Year End

	2004	2003	2002
Banks			
CIBC	$73.00	$59.21	$38.75
TD Financial	48.98	43.86	29.35
Bank of Montreal	57.55	49.33	38.10
Royal Bank of Canada	63.40	63.48	54.41
Bank of Nova Scotia	39.60	65.47	45.88
Insurance			
Sun Life	40.15	32.87	26.71
Manulife	55.40	41.85	34.39
Great West Lifeco	26.70	22.75	18.63
Mutual Fund Companies			
CI Funds	14.04	10.00	11.89
Investors Group	36.64	31.05	26.75
Integrated Oils			
Imperial Oil	71.15	57.53	44.86
PetroCanada	61.17	63.91	48.91
Shell Canada	79.99	61.25	49.20
Railroads			
CNR	73.07	82.00	65.23
CPR	41.10	36.58	31.15
Resource/Mining			
Finning	34.99	30.00	25.55
Teck-Cominco	36.92	21.93	11.60
Miscellaneous			
Loblaw	72.02	67.85	54.00
Magna International (US)	98.57	104.04	88.07
Saputo	36.15	33.05	22.50
Prospects			
TransCanada Pipelines	29.80	27.88	22.92
Atco	58.50	48.00	43.00
TransAlta	18.05	18.53	17.11

Figure 5-4

Cardinal Rules

Potential Stock Picks for 2005

Dividend Payout Ratio

	2004	2003	2002	2001	2000	Average
Banks						
CIBC	39.8%	31.7%	118.5%	34.9%	26.3%	38.7%
TD Financial	40.1	76.8	-448.0	53.2	60.1	68.7
Bank of Montreal	33.9	37.5	44.0	41.0	30.5	36.8
Royal Bank of Canada	47.8	39.2	38.7	39.2	32.5	39.7
Bank of Nova Scotia	39.0	35.9	44.2	30.7	27.6	35.6
Insurance						
Sun Life	30.8	31.6	30.6	23.2	0.0	25.0
Manulife	26.0	23.6	20.8	20.2	13.5	21.5
Great West Lifeco	38.5	38.5	37.8	56.1	37.8	40.3
Mutual Fund Companies						
CI Funds	49.4	93.5	-17.1	83.3	0.0	95.8
Investors Group	51.3	48.8	46.5	69.5	45.2	50.9
Integrated Oils						
Imperial Oil	15.3	150.0	26.3	26.7	23.1	26.3
PetroCanada	9.2	6.5	11.1	10.9	12.7	9.5
Shell Canada	20.3	28.1	39.6	21.9	25.0	25.3
Railroads						
CNR	18.0	19.1	21.6	0.0	0.0	19.3
CPR	20.0	20.2	16.7	0.0	0.0	18.8
Resource/Mining						
Finning	28.0	21.4	17.8	14.9	21.3	20.6
Teck-Cominco	10.0	29.4	333.3	-117.6	30.3	26.1
Miscellaneous						
Loblaw	21.7	19.7	18.3	19.6	23.4	20.4
Magna International (US)	20.8	26.2	23.5	21.9	19.3	22.1
Saputo	27.3	23.6	26.0	0.0	0.0	25.6
Prospects						
TransCanada Pipelines	54.7	61.0	64.5	69.2	55.2	60.3
Atco	26.2	27.3	21.2	24.9	24.3	24.7
TransAlta	113.6	79.4	85.5	78.7	60.2	80.1
Average	33.7	42.6	22.9	30.9	30.1	36.1

Figure 5-6

Cardinal Rules

Potential Stock Picks for 2005

P/E Ratio (trailing)

	2004	2003	2002
Banks			
CIBC	13.2	11.4	28.7
TD Financial	14.4	29.0	-117.4
Bank of Montreal	13.0	14.3	14.2
Royal Bank of Canada	15.0	14.5	13.8
Bank of Nova Scotia	14.0	28.0	27.8
Insurance			
Sun Life	14.4	15.3	14.6
Manulife	15.3	12.6	11.9
Great West Lifeco	15.0	15.6	14.9
Mutual Fund Companies			
CI Funds	17.1	32.3	-34.0
Investors Group	16.4	15.3	14.5
Integrated Oils			
Imperial Oil	12.4	99.2	14.0
PetroCanada	9.3	10.4	13.6
Shell Canada	17.2	21.0	24.4
Railroads			
CNR	16.8	23.5	24.6
CPR	15.8	14.5	10.2
Resource/Mining			
Finning	24.5	17.9	15.1
Teck-Cominco	12.3	32.3	193.3
Miscellaneous			
Loblaw	20.5	22.2	20.6
Magna International (US)	13.8	20.0	15.2
Saputo	16.4	16.3	14.6
Prospects			
TransCanada Pipelines	13.9	15.8	14.8
Atco	10.9	10.9	7.8
TransAlta	20.5	14.7	14.6
Average	15.3	22.0	16.2

Figure 5-7

Cardinal Rules

Potential Stock Picks for 2005

	Normalized EPS End 2004	Normalized P/E End 2004
Banks		
CIBC	$4.22	17.3
TD Financial	1.65	29.8
Bank of Montreal	3.29	17.5
Royal Bank of Canada	3.92	16.2
Bank of Nova Scotia	2.13	18.6
Insurance		
Sun Life	2.06	19.5
Manulife	2.88	19.2
Great West Lifeco	1.21	22.1
Mutual Fund Companies		
CI Funds	0.21	66.9
Investors Group	1.70	21.5
Integrated Oils		
Imperial Oil	3.20	22.2
PetroCanada	4.63	13.2
Shell Canada	3.25	24.6
Railroads		
CNR	3.49	20.9
CPR	2.74	15.0
Resource/Mining		
Finning	1.42	24.7
Teck-Cominco	0.84	43.7
Miscellaneous		
Loblaw	2.59	27.8
Magna International (US)	6.15	16.0
Saputo	1.57	23.1
Prospects		
TransCanada Pipelines	1.64	18.1
Atco	4.63	12.6
TransAlta	1.25	14.5

CHAPTER SIX

Who Is This Clark Kent?

The Cardinal Rules for investing seem almost mundane when considered against the backdrop of daily business headlines and TV's talking heads touting the latest news on the next big thing in investing. Isn't investing the high-pressure, thrill-a-minute kind of life that we see in the movies? Sure, in the worlds of investment-banking and in mergers and acquisitions you will find some wheeler-dealers, maybe even some driving Porsches and dating Sharon Stone look-alikes, but that's not the real world of asset management. Asset management is a much slower, considered business that should aim at stewardship and prudence.

Asset management is about care-taking. I personally don't want a flashy character in a Porsche managing my mother's money, or even my own for that matter. In a market of stocks, I want a careful, deliberate, cautious manager for most of my money. I want Father Knows Best, not James Bond! I want somebody kicking tires, going over financials, checking out the management and seriously considering all aspects of a business before I invest in it.

This may not sync with the media-popular image of the brilliant young stock broker, but it is how the great masters of the past have practiced the art of asset management. It's from that school of value investment that the Cardinal Rules were devised. In fact, Tim Burt, Mr. Cardinal himself, spent eight years teaching finance and investments at the University of Manitoba even while he was managing the assets that generated the tremendous track record of returns that we see today. Of course he taught investing like he practices it, the value way instead of the TV way.

In a small but diverse community such as Winnipeg, where Cardinal Capital is based, the range of clients is not terribly broad. Professionals, white and blue-collar workers, business owners and farmers make up the bulk of Cardinal's individual clientele, and pension plans and charities are their institutional clients. Many individual clients qualify for the role of "Millionaire Next Door" in that, by and large, they are not visibly wealthy but have saved and lived prudently. Not for them the flashy, dizzying world of high finance and get-rich-quick. Instead they have opted for the cautious prudence of Tim Burt and the Cardinal Rules and, in general, this choice has paid off handsomely for them. Many of Tim's long-time clients have retired now, with Cardinal portfolio-financed motor homes or winter residences. For them, the worries that we relative youngsters face are generally over and done with. They've earned their peace of mind.

Tim is gratified that he has been able to have a positive impact on the lives of so many of his clients. He also regrets that a few clients from the early days directed him to restrict their portfolios to bond investments only. Now those clients are taking income at the same level as they were in earlier days (when higher interest rates prevailed) and he is seeing their capital diminish. On the other hand, he sees clients that started with him in the "early days" and both he and they have trouble believing that they are now multi-millionaires as a result of his efforts.

Tim is adamant that equities make a world of difference in how wealthy his clients get. Today he gets cards in the winter from clients on tropical beaches (not an uncommon practice for Winnipeg residents who can afford it) thanking him, because without him such trips would not be possible. That reinforces his feeling about the magic of compounding and the need for equities. He looks at charts showing the progress of those clients who have taken little or no income, and compares them to clients who have regularly taken significant income. Those who reinvested are head and shoulders above those who didn't.

Everyone's heard of the Oracle of Omaha and the Wizards of Wall Street. Very few have heard of Tim Burt (the Winnipeg Whiz?). Who is he? What influenced, trained, molded him into the super-investor that he is today? When you meet Tim Burt for the first time it is not unlike how I imagine it would be meeting Clark Kent, knowing him to be Superman. You are surprised by the humble demeanour, expecting more because of the achievements. While meek is not a word I could use to describe Tim, he is certainly mild-mannered and soft-spoken, not unlike Clark Kent. Quite unassuming, he has the quiet confidence of one who has proven his abilities and who has pride in his accomplishments. He has the precision of an academic in discussions and is rather rigorous in his choice of phrases and in expressing his ideas. His office is uncluttered, but it does have stacks of papers, old research reports and old annual reports, both on shelves and in out-of-the-way floor-space, obviously one of our generation who is still more comfortable with paper than with laptops. It is no surprise that this person is an exceptional securities analyst, but it is unexpected that he founded an independent portfolio investment firm in Winnipeg, so far from his mid-western U.S. roots. Despite his recent fascination with acquiring and riding motorcycles, Tim doesn't strike you as a risk-taker or an entrepreneur, so you might wonder what encouraged him to take the leap into starting a business in the high-risk area of equity investment management.

THE ACADEMIC INVESTOR

Originally from Illinois, where he took undergraduate and Master's degrees in Finance (majoring in Securities Analysis) at the University of Illinois, Tim wanted to be a professor of finance and teach Securities Analysis at a good college in the Midwest. That was his early and primary career ambition. It was only in wilder moments that he considered a career as a money manager, and that was usually when his anxiety about public speaking overwhelmed him. Tim was educated in the value tradition of Benjamin Graham and David Dodd and became an early fan of Warren Buffett, but he was a voracious reader of anything pertaining to the Stock Market. After doing his graduate work in Illinois, the writings of Peter Lynch and David Dreman extended his knowledge and understanding of value investing. (In those early years Tim failed to note Dreman's Winnipeg connection and saw no premonition of Winnipeg in his future.) The preaching of Warren Buffett left Tim with a deep belief in quality as the overriding criterion for stock selection and Dreman's contrarian philosophy won him over to the importance of buying at low prices to achieve good returns and protect capital. In more recent years, when teaching at the University of Manitoba, it was only half in jest that Tim would start off each new class of aspiring analysts with the announcement that this was "Course 9.342: Religious Studies in Finance," where one would learn that although there were many strategies for investment management, here they would learn only "the one, true philosophy of securities analysis."

In conversation it quickly becomes apparent that Tim is passionate about his profession of investment manager, despite his earlier career choice to become an academic. It was his poor fortune, and our good one, that started him on the road to independent money management. While an enthusiastic research assistant studying towards his Ph.D. and preparing for a career as a university professor, a soon-to-be-unemployed pregnant wife necessitated that Tim take on the role of breadwinner instead of continuing to depend on the largesse of his wife for the family income. Tim left school, joining a small Midwestern bank as an investment officer, taking on client work and helping trade securities for client portfolios. To help ends meet and because of Tim's hopes for a teaching career, he also managed to secure a part-time position teaching economics and business at a local community college. He overcame his natural shyness and improved his lecture style by participating in Toastmasters and the Dale Carnegie course in public speaking.

Many Ph.D. students would have borrowed money to continue on the academic path, but Tim's true risk-averse nature came to the fore in this instance, and often in later years. He would not take on massive student debt with the risk inherent in that path, choosing instead the prudent route of secure employment. However, he didn't find the bank position particularly fulfilling and after two years there and with a second child on the way, Tim found a position with a St. Louis brokerage firm as a research analyst. It was here that his eyes were really opened to how the world worked and how this esoteric profession of Securities Analysis was practiced.

HONING THE SKILLS FOR VALUE INVESTING

As a research analyst, Tim took on the analysis of U.S. firms located in the Midwest for inclusion in portfolios. He started developing the diligent and systematic approaches that Buffett, Lynch, Dreman et. al. had persuaded him were necessary to properly analyse securities. He was surprised to find that this methodology was not the norm. He did site visits, researched management, had discussions with corporate officers and found that he totally enjoyed the experience and that it fed his passion for "doing it right." His expertise in analysis was gradually honed and his personal philosophy towards investing started to gel. His aversion to small cap stocks developed during this period, as did his preference for large cap, dividend-paying stocks. Much of his research was into small-cap stocks at this time, but because of their usually illiquid nature and sporadic following, he noted that their market behaviour was far less predictable or rational than even the market as a whole. Again, being naturally risk averse and finding that the predictable, boring large cap stocks could provide more than adequate returns (particularly when adjusted for volatility), Tim gravitated towards research in this area. It was about this time that the teaching career started to be seen only as an option, rather than the must-do choice of earlier years. This penchant for analysis, which Tim had hoped to enjoy as a hobby while teaching, could actually be a career in its own right. Tim's interest was piqued.

When his employer was sold to a national brokerage firm that had their own team of analysts, Tim's future again became cloudy and a job in Minneapolis as director of corporate finance, researching and preparing IPOs, was the result. His numerical skills and market knowledge were valuable in this role, but the job was not teaching nor was it securities analysis. Tim was disappointed, but it paid the bills, bought time until he could earn his CFA, and serendipitously, put him in contact with an affable neighbour, a medical doctor who had moved to the Twin Cities from Winnipeg, Manitoba.

Winnipeg was a place totally out of mind for Tim, who still wanted to finish his doctorate at a good Midwestern school. Yet, when Tim chatted with the doctor about his disappointment in his career and bemoaned the fact that national U.S. brokers did not hire analysts from regional firms, the doctor pointed out that Canada had its own, unique investment industry, and in addition there was a good chance that Tim's American experience would be viewed as a valuable asset there. Of course, Tim had no interest in moving to Winnipeg, but the demands of the job with its IPO-driven existence wore on him and he became increasingly frustrated at his inability to progress towards his own career objectives. The doctor persisted until Tim, in a futile gesture probably intended to close a door, forwarded his resume to

Richardson Securities in Winnipeg, with a request to be considered for any analyst position they might have open. To his great surprise, this resulted in an interview in Winnipeg in February of 1980 and a position starting the following May as Richardson's senior U.S. equity analyst.

In this role, Tim refined and enhanced his securities analysis methodology, and he began to consider portfolio construction, that is, how to fit his recommended stock picks into a portfolio that protected capital and moderated volatility. Richardson soon merged with Greenshields securities (becoming Richardson-Greenshields, or Rich-Green in industry parlance, in 1982) and Tim became responsible for providing research on U.S. equities to a national network of stock-brokers and clients. When on speaking tours Tim was asked by brokers and clients to comment about one U.S. firm after another. He soon found that he had become a generalist, with expertise in industry after industry, but with an approach and a methodology that could be applied to virtually any firm in any industry except, to Rich-Green's dismay, to technology.

Tim's analysis of technology firms in the early 1980s persuaded him that investing in that sector was a pure crapshoot. He could find no consistent impartial way to establish the intrinsic value of technology firms without a deep understanding of the technology involved. And even when the technology was understandable, a firm could bypass, acquire or leapfrog technical deficiencies or competitors at what seemed like the drop of a hat. Relying on Buffettology – don't invest in what you can't understand – Tim veered away from recommending technology stocks (and generally still does).

During this stage of his career, Tim was active in developing new talent at Rich-Green and was also a driving force behind the Winnipeg chapter of the Society of Financial Analysts. I have since bumped into many analysts across the country who know Tim from his activities during those days.

MANAGING OTHER PEOPLE'S MONEY

Having become an acknowledged expert analyst of U.S. equities, Tim now hungered to be a money manager — the trigger-puller that took the results of securities analysis one step further and actually used the resulting recommendations to make money for clients. Now with a family of three children who had developed a fondness for Winnipeg, Tim hoped that he might soon get employment as a money manager at a Winnipeg company. In fact, Investors Syndicate was on the top of his wish list. But when he was offered the opportunity to manage U.S. equities for the large and secure London Life, the bird in the hand was irresistible. London, Ontario, was smaller than Winnipeg and seemed to be an ideal place to raise a family. In June of 1986 he joined London Life.

This led to the first of two events that shaped Tim's investing strategy and reinforced his faith in the philosophy that he had developed. Tim began by setting up trading, custody and brokerage arrangements for his portfolio in London; by the fall of 1986 he had the portfolio positioned and proceeded to watch its value soar as the stock market in the U.S. roared upwards. By August of 1987, Tim was astounded at what the market was offering for many of his holdings and at the levels the markets in general had reached. Sensing that values were far higher than they should be, Tim sold and trimmed many of the holdings and looked for places where good value might be obtained. By October his portfolio was more than 35% cash, and Tim was on one of his trips to New York City to visit with his brokerage firms. As a special treat, Goldman Sachs had scheduled a floor tour of the New York Stock Exchange with a floor trader for Monday, October 19th, 1987.

SHAPED BY THE CRASH OF '87

The market had declined on Friday the 16th and expectations for Monday were tentative. As Tim's tour progressed he sensed an increasing tension on the floor. His guiding floor trader begged off the tour midway through and then a general announcement was made asking all visitors to leave. As Tim watched, a gaggle of Japanese tourists who spoke no English were asked to leave by security guards who spoke no Japanese, an amusing interlude in an otherwise frantic tableau. Outside the exchange a press of media had converged on the exchange steps and the magnitude of the events of the day became clear. Tim had witnessed first hand the Crash of '87.

Tim spent the remainder of that week in New York and what made a lasting impression on him was that the gloom and desolation that he saw within the investment community contrasted markedly from the sentiment outside that community. He vividly remembers watching an aerospace/defense industry analyst break down in tears before a red screen of decimated share prices, proclaiming, "This is the end. It's all over!" He also remembers sitting with a very senior economist/strategist who advised him to learn a new trade since there wouldn't be any jobs in the investment industry for at least a decade. The man believed they were entering a massive deflationary depression that would be a repeat of the Dirty Thirties.

Tim didn't quite see it that way. Sitting on a war chest of 35% cash, old risk-averse Tim returned to southern Ontario and perused the shopping malls. They were full to bursting as the late stages of a massive real estate boom fuelled optimism and consumer spending. Acquaintances, neighbours and parents of children's schoolmates unanimously informed him that the stock market crash might be a big deal for Bay Street, but that it didn't affect them significantly. Tim's initial reaction to the crash – that this was a once in a lifetime buying opportunity – was reinforced. By early November he was buying and within two weeks his portfolio was again fully invested. With the market recovery came tremendous performance for his portfolio, especially since he had dodged a good portion of the October debacle. For the calendar year 1987 his portfolio was ranked by SEI, a U.S.

based investment consulting firm, as in the top one percent of U.S. equity funds.

Tim's success confirmed for him that his methodology provided him with information that was far more reliable than the market's groupthink. From that point forward he would know that if he had confidence in his analysis, he could take his own path on buying or selling and not feel pressured to kowtow to the market's assessment of valuations. On the flip-side Tim saw billions of dollars of investors' worth destroyed in a matter of hours that October. As a result, the responsibility for client money is a burden that he feels heavily, and he constantly acts to avoid risks, seeing his primary role, like a physician, to "First, do no harm!"

LEARNING FROM A CRISIS

The second formative event in Tim's early career was during the so-called Savings & Loan Crisis of 1990-1991. Tim's portfolio was heavily tilted to the financial services industry, although his analysis had kept him clear of the S&L and trust sector that experienced the bankruptcies and turmoil throughout the crisis. Despite the fact that the problems were not in his own holdings, the collateral damage to their value was extensive. The large exposure to financials did result in his portfolio performance being terrible over that period, even though his methodology pointed out to him that his specific holdings should not be experiencing the devaluations that occurred. Several of Tim's holdings were in banking entities known as "super-regionals" and many of them were fairly illiquid, even trading on the "over-the-counter" market rather than through a stock exchange. This made it very difficult for Tim to sell and exacerbated the portfolio's difficulties. Price quotes were often very thin; on some occasions there were no bids on certain holdings. The situation resulted in a number of sleepless nights for Tim and he believes it was probably one of the most emotionally trying professional experiences he has had.

However, this experience reminded Tim, firstly, of the importance of diversification by sector, even though the individual holdings might be carefully selected and correct in their own right and, secondly, of the importance of liquidity. Never get into a holding that you can't get out of when you want to. The Cardinal Rules were gradually taking form and being forged in the furnace of market experience.

After five years running the London Life portfolio, Tim had developed his systems and his confidence to the extent that he felt he had what it takes to be his own boss in managing money. At London Life new policies were being introduced relating to the use of derivative securities to insure a portfolio. Tim found that researching or determining the derivative position became a major distraction from the security selection. The derivative position was not particularly amenable to a value analysis, and being a value disciple, he was not comfortable in adding them to the portfolio. An idea that had been germinating for the past few years started to grow— perhaps it was time to hang out his own shingle.

STRIKING OUT ON HIS OWN

On the family front, London had been a bit of a disappointment. Because London was an old community of old families, the result was the Burts never truly felt a part of the community. Their social circle was London Life. They lived in a neighbourhood where white collar, branch-plant management employees rotated in for a few years before moving on to other locations. The U.S. beckoned. Tim's mother and a sister lived in Pacific Grove, California, and the climate and economic growth rates were attractive. Tim actively prepared to move south and strike out on his own. Of course, the Richardson-Greenshields and London Life names would be meaningless in terms of recognition and credibility to most Californians. He also realized that going out on your own in the U.S. meant that health-care could be a huge liability if any health issues arose with the children. Ever the risk avoider, Tim shied away from signing the lease he had negotiated in Pacific Grove. The Burts thought back to their Winnipeg years and the network that Tim had developed through the Rich-Green years. In the summer of 1992, they packed up the three kids and moved back to Winnipeg, where Tim founded Cardinal Capital Management.

For Tim, founding Cardinal was an adventurous, aggressive step in what had been a cautious, careful career. The step was disastrous. Tim learned that institutions would not deal with an unproven, individual manager. He learned that Canadians wanted to invest in Canadian, not U.S. equities. He learned that his network at Rich-Green was not supportive of an outside-the-firm manager. He learned that he had better take a job teaching at the University of Manitoba and start reading the Globe and Mail as well as the Wall Street Journal.

It was a slow start. Rather than buying a house, the family rented. Gradually his client base grew. Tim developed a relationship with two financial planners who believed in the Warren Buffett value philosophy that Tim had enhanced, and eventually referrals started to trickle in. As the firm's revenue grew, Tim had to spend it almost as fast as it came in. Kelly Berg, his original administrative assistant, was hired. Tony Demarin, who had worked for a corporate client of Tim's in the Rich-Green days, was hired as an assistant portfolio manager in 1999 (in time to learn from the TransCanada coup). Over the next few years, working together with Tony, the Cardinal Rules were refined. Tony is now a fully qualified portfolio manager and partner. Cardinal has grown organically to the point that there are a total of fourteen employees, including three additional investment analysts, as well as three clerical staff and in-house legal counsel. Both Tony and Tim independently manage the portfolios using Cardinal's established philosophy and process. Tim continues to reinvest revenue to enhance Cardinal's capabilities in terms of research access, personnel strength and service. With over $500 million under management and a 12-year track record in Canadian and Foreign equities, Cardinal definitely has all the credentials needed to break onto the national scene, but the firm is still a jewel relatively unknown outside of Winnipeg. To a large degree, this flows from Tim's personality. Still fairly shy and retiring, he does little to promote himself or his company. As his track record demonstrates; he prefers numbers to people; he remains Clark Kent.

STILL A CLARK KENT

This is not to say that Tim doesn't like people. His employees love working with him and for him. In his teaching days (now long past, since Cardinal now requires all his attention) his students consistently applauded his classes. Even now Tim personally writes quarterly to his clients, generally providing comfort in a world that thrives on discomfort. I've read a number of financial newsletters and Tim's is the only one I am aware of where an investment advisor actually counsels his clients when it is a good time to withdraw some capital and splurge on a new car. When you ask him about this, he responds that he sees too many clients who have money and who are afraid to spend it. Often an independent professional advising them that it is ok to spend is the catalyst that they need to enjoy their money.

Kelly Berg tells the story of one client, a very shy woman, who took Tim at his word when he suggested that clients consider buying a new car. Tim actually spent a half day with her, visiting various dealerships, viewing different models and talking with salespeople. Tim is still hurt that her choice involved buying a vehicle from the nicest salesperson! "Oh well," he says, "having wealth gives you the freedom to make your own choices."

ENJOYING YOUR MONEY WHILE YOU CAN

Tim tells the story of an uncle who died of cancer as a relatively young man in his mid-sixties. This uncle had owned a Ford LTD for fifteen years and had subsequently owned a Camry and an Accord, but he had always dreamed of owning a Mercedes Benz. Three months before his death Tim visited him and his uncle indicated that if he could do it over again he would travel more and buy that Mercedes. After his death, Tim was shocked to learn that his uncle had a great deal of wealth and really had no financial reason not to have bought a Mercedes. Because Tim is so vitally concerned about his clients, he sees part of his role being to counsel them about using their money. "What's money for? You earn it, and you defer buying to save it, so why not enjoy what it can do instead of leaving it all to somebody after you die?" says Tim.

Tim's clients obviously appreciate his attention and genuine concern for them. Eighty per cent of his original clients are still with him. He regularly gets cards and letters from them, thanking him and reporting on their personal lives. In Cardinal's early years, when Tim was desperate to build his business and living off the proceeds of the sale of his London home, the minimum client account size was officially $150,000. Several of his early clients came in at that low level and are now worth up to $2,000,000. Another client has an account that is worth slightly more than its original value, but two times its original value has been withdrawn. Many of those early clients have retired either early or on their own schedule, benefiting from the growth and security of their Cardinal investments. Some have retired in their fifties, some as early as fifty-two years of age. They can buy motor homes and spend winters in the southern U.S. or Mexico. At least one client spends four to six months a year in southern Europe and another withdrew funds to buy and renovate a small duplex and now largely travels the world. For people so inclined, what an idyllic existence! Tim takes great pride in the fact that his work provides the wherewithal for clients to achieve their dreams, to live the fullest possible lives. Isn't that why we are all working and saving?

OVERCOMING STOCK MARKET FEARS

Given his faith and his track record, it is understandable that Tim cannot contemplate that investors would be afraid of investing in the stock market. Some perma-bears harp constantly on the crash of 1987 and the bear markets of 1973-74 without acknowledging that despite these interruptions equity markets have returned an average of about 12% per annum over the last half century. Tim cannot conceive of going through life worrying about what might happen to stock prices. He believes that an innate optimism is essential to be an investor, and to be healthy and happy in life. The world's economy is expanding, and as its inhabitants strive to provide themselves and their descendants a better life, it will continue to expand and improve. He sees the development and growth of a middle class in India and China as a key trend which will continue into the future, and one that demonstrates that, overall, the planet has improved from the time when those two countries were in a constant battle against mass starvation.

Tim's optimism leads him to view the future of investing as a world of "portfolios without borders." He laments the practice of establishing Canadian or U.S. or European equity mandates, instead of just a mandate to buy good stocks. His comfort in the international securities arena is reflected in Cardinal's success with its foreign equity portfolios. Buying steel stocks in Korea or consumer goods stocks in Europe are all part and parcel of his job; each requires the same in-depth analysis and familiarity that Tim believes necessary for any investment.

When asked why other investors don't do as well as Cardinal does, especially when the rules are so simple, Tim responds, "The rules are so simple, anybody can do it. But the process is hard, unless you have a passion for it. Reading annual reports and financial statements is really boring, dry work." That is the essence of genuine success in investing. The first four personality traits of a good fund manager according to international value manager, Peter Cundill, are:

dedication, passion, intelligence and discipline. As Tim says, you really need a passion for this to do it well, and you need discipline to keep it all under control. Not many people have that temperament. Tim's passion is for assessing the worth of a company and then comparing that to how the market values it. Curiosity drives him to understand how the differences arise, and his knowledge of the fallibility of the market, proven in October 1987, help him believe that his assessment could well be more correct than the market's. In contrast to the many larger-than-life personalities featured in the financial news, he is a relative wallflower – but one with a Superman record.

CHAPTER SEVEN

How The Rich
Get Richer

Up till now the Cardinal Rules have been used by Tim and his team for the benefit of their clients, but unfortunately not just anybody can become a client. Like any business, Cardinal has to be efficient and not get bogged down in expensive paperwork. Any activity they undertake must cost less than it earns in revenue. For this reason, Cardinal has a minimum account size of $500,000 and a minimum fee of $5,000 per year. Many of us might be getting close to accumulating that level of wealth as we approach retirement, but we may not be quite there yet, and lots of us aren't even close. Cardinal's high net worth (HNW) clients — institutions and endowments and the select wealthy few — have some advantages in dealing with their investment managers, and they generally have several expectations in terms of service and reporting. If we look at how the millionaire clients manage their investments, maybe we can learn a thing or two that will lead us also on the path towards more wealth.

INVESTING LIKE A MILLIONAIRE

Probably one of the most crucial differences for wealthy as opposed to small investors is in how the Investment Committees at institutions or the HNW clients approach their investments. We should all take a lesson from them. They usually treat their investment portfolio like a business and, by and large, they contract out the management of that business. They do a search and a performance review of several managers before they contract with one or two in selected asset classes. And, like any other business relationship, the contract is in writing and spells out the responsibilities of both parties. Sounds logical, doesn't it. But so many of us smaller investors just say, "What should I buy and where do I sign?"

Note that this does not mean that the institution or HNW client hands over responsibility for the portfolio to another party. Tempting as it sometimes is, you can't just wash your hands of responsibility and say, "You do it!" Someone at the institution or in the wealthy client's family must provide strategic direction and set objectives for the manager, just as one would for a building manager if one had real estate investments or for a business manager if one owned a business. If an owner-manager is personally running a business, then he or she generally has little time to also oversee an investment portfolio; nor do they generally think they have the expertise to do so. They are used to hiring specialist professionals to do the jobs that need doing, and an investment manager is just another one of these.

The services contract will outline the expectations, the commitments, the duties and responsibilities, and the price that will be charged and terms of payment. In the case of institutional or HNW investment management, the contract generally includes an Investment Policy Statement (IPS) through which the investor indicates his or her expectations of the portfolio in terms of income and volatility, and describes the asset class universe that he wants the portfolio manager to manage within. If there are restrictions on the manager's activities and investments, they will be described in the IPS. Often a manager is restricted from participating in securities or financial arrangements that the investor believes are too risky or that are precluded by the institution's by-laws or regulations. Otherwise, there is a danger that the portfolio manager take on inappropriate risk in order to try to realize exceptional returns.

The client's expectations are usually determined through a risk tolerance evaluation and an asset allocation process. The investment manager may provide historical data to show how a similar portfolio behaved in the past, however, in the investment industry it is illegal to commit to future performance of an equity portfolio (not to mention unrealistic). History is only a guide and the actual ongoing performance may be considerably different than historical results. This fact must be understood by all parties, whether we are talking about institutions, HNW clients or the smallest of small investors.

CAPITALIZING ON THE TAX LAWS

Since most HNW investors own assets outside of an RSP or pension, and are in the highest tax bracket, the tax treatment of investment returns is crucial to the private investor. This is less so for institutions, which are often not taxed. Managers such as Cardinal, who favour dividend-earning securities, are often chosen for a significant portion of an investor's Canadian wealth because the tax laws in Canada favour dividend income over interest and regular income. Managers like Cardinal who have a "hold-the-winners, sell-the-losers" strategy also minimize ongoing capital gains tax which benefits HNW investors. If you own investments outside of an RSP you should also be concerned with this element of your portfolio, since taxes are that unavoidable issue that can negatively impact on our investing success.

On that note, the Income Tax Act allows for many portfolio management fees and expenses to be deducted from investment income. HNW investors usually receive an explicit statement of expenses charged to them, and they in turn deduct these fees on their income tax returns. Many financial salespeople make a big deal out of this feature, presenting it as a great advantage for their own products. In reality, it is not such a big issue. If a $100,000 investment makes 12% ($12,000) before fees and then 2% is paid in fees, taxable income is $10,000. If mutual funds and other like products make 12% before costs, they deduct the costs before they calculate the unit price and the client only sees and reports the net income of $10,000.

Institutions and HNW investors generally are very concerned with security — personal and financial — as we all should be. They generally want their assets held in a very secure, reputable institution. The big brokerage houses — which in Canada are now largely affiliated with the large Schedule A banks — act as stockbrokers and also perform custodial services, holding and securing assets for clients, both individual and institutional. Thus managers for wealthy investors such as Cardinal will allow clients to select which brokerage house they wish to have as custodian of their assets, and then the client assigns trading authority on the account to Cardinal. The brokerage house thus receives all instructions on the account from Cardinal and this relationship will continue until the client wishes to change it. In this way, HNW clients are assured that a major and stable institution, which is subject to extensive regulation and governance, is responsible for the physical caretaking of their investments, while they are still able to take advantage of the expertise of a portfolio manager of their own choosing.

MEASURING YOUR INVESTMENT MANAGER'S PERFORMANCE

Just as an employer evaluates a manager based on performance, institutions and other millionaire clients insist on being informed about the activities of their portfolio manager. In general, most institutional investors and HNW clients demand reports on a quarterly, or sometimes semi-annual, basis, depending on the client needs and their level of comfort with their portfolio manager. Institutions, and to a lesser extent HNW clients, expect these reports to contain a list of holdings and a measure of performance relative to the expectations laid out in the IPS. Since the IPS lays out expectations for risk and return, and since the reports are used to assess the performance of the manager, it is only natural that such information be required by the investor.

There is no reason why smaller, or less wealthy investors, should not also insist on this type of reporting. If our job is to provide direction and evaluate results, we need to receive the information necessary to do this. A quarterly time frame is frequent enough to allow the investor to properly evaluate the manager, but not so frequent that it results in excessive paperwork and extra costs. Through these reports HNW clients can assess whether the manager is adhering to the principles and constraints of the IPS.

In addition to this, securities rules in Canada dictate that buy and sell activities be confirmed through immediate reports to the clients. In other words, this must be done, although for managed portfolios like those of Cardinal's HNW clients, it is done by the custodian of the assets. The regulator's intent with such reporting is to allow clients to catch broker error or unauthorized trades, but it also allows investors to check up on their brokers' activities.

It is important to note that because the volatility and return of various asset classes vary considerably through time, it is not very useful to look at the volatility and return of an investment portfolio in isolation from the performance of its universe. Just as one cannot assess a building manager's performance without considering the existence of rent controls or a massive price change in heating costs, one cannot judge a portfolio manager without considering what has happened in the external environment affecting the asset class in which he invests. This is one of the reasons the investment industry developed the various indices to benchmark the performance of several distinct asset classes. It is only when the portfolio manager's results are viewed in relation to the relevant indices that a client gets a meaningful measure of the manager's performance. This is why an IPS usually dictates the benchmarks that a manager will be compared to, and these benchmarks should be included in the reports on the performance of the portfolio.

So this is the level of service and structure of management that is demanded by most millionaire clients and, with a minimum account size of $500,000, Cardinal can be profitable providing it for a management fee starting at 1.5% of the portfolio.

HNW SERVICE WITHOUT HNW ASSETS
Unfortunately, most of us have trouble scraping together enough money for this year's RSP contribution, let alone $500,000 to meet Cardinal's minimum account requirements. Yet for those of us at the leading edge of the baby-boom, whose retirement years are fast approaching and who have neither the time nor the inclinations to manage our own money, we really need the premium returns that equities can provide along with the security of shock-resistant investments managed under the Cardinal Rules. What is a lesser-net-worth investor to do?

This is why we at Value Partners have designed a platform whereby the smaller investor can utilize Cardinal's expertise and receive the service and treatment that are usually only available to HNW clients.

By and large, investors in Canada with smaller portfolios who want to access equity markets are limited to using mutual funds, (or segregated funds if issued through an insurance company), or a variety of wrap products from the brokerage industry. While many of these are excellent products, they often have a fairly large management expense ratio, due in part to the high administrative costs of dealing with smaller investment amounts. Often they are fairly opportunistic in how they are managed and, because marketing is a key element for growth with most mutual fund and other wealth management companies, managers are often pulled toward hot sectors, hot styles and esoteric strategies that advertise well. Boring, plain old vanilla-style Cardinal Rules-type management doesn't lead to exciting sales stories.

Value Partners Investments Inc.

Because we believe so strongly in the Cardinal Rules and their results, and recognize that a growing group of Canadian investors need the results that the Cardinal Rules can bring, Value Partners Investments Inc. (VPII) working with Cardinal Capital Management have developed a limited number of fund products through which Cardinal management will be available to smaller portfolios at a reasonable cost. With these products we have also tried to present the type of service and reporting that a millionaire client would insist on, so that less wealthy investors can manage their wealth like a millionaire institution does.

By setting the minimum account size at $25,000 we eliminate a number of the high administrative costs associated with thousands of small clients. And, by limiting the investment products to a small number with only one type of distribution structure, we reduce administrative costs further. Of course, this means that it won't be a mutual fund that responds to every hot stock that comes along, but it also means that investors can have the confidence of knowing the investment strategy is based on the Cardinal Rules rather than on a variety of mandates and styles. By the innovative use of technology we can also provide clients with a personalized IPS, and with quarterly performance reporting detailing individual holdings. At the same time, the custodial capabilities and security of the Royal Bank of Canada will provide investors with the assurance of a secure custodian. All of this results in a management fee of 1.8% and a targeted management expense ratio of just over 2%. For larger accounts, over

$250,000, this fee can be reduced further to 1.5%.

Value Partners Investments Inc. (VPII) is offering Cardinal Capital Management pools directed at Canadian equity, foreign equity and Canadian income mandates. I have a minor ownership interest in VPII, and some of my partners in the venture also own an interest in Cardinal Capital Management. It is for this reason that VPII has been able to contract with Cardinal Capital and Tim Burt to manage these funds, and why we are confident that we can retain Tim's services into the foreseeable future. All in all, it's a very exciting venture for us and we all believe it can make a huge difference in the wealth of the mature Canadians who need it most.

CHAPTER EIGHT

Taking Control and Getting Started

"OK, I've read the rules. I understand them and I think they make sense. What do I do now?" Great question. If you're like me, there's a real danger that ten years from now you will be in exactly the same situation you are today but thinking, "I really should have done something!" And we all know how fast ten years can fly by! The time for procrastination is over. My efforts in writing this book will go for naught if I haven't inspired you to start taking action today to achieve where you want to be in ten years. Apparently it wasn't Yogi Berra who said, "If you don't know where you wanna go, you'll never get there," but it could have been!

THE "BURNED" AND "ABOUT TO BE BURNED"

In my experience, I've come across two general types of investors who need to consider the Cardinal Rules now. I categorize them as the "Burned" and the "About-To-Be-Burned." The Burned are that group who sometime in the past were hurt by equity market declines, frauds or failures, and are now so fearful of equities that they are trapped in the safe investments like GICs. The About-To-Be-Burned are those who are invested in scattered portfolios that are running on autopilot.

They have experienced the market's gyrations and bought into the "buy and hold" mantra, hoping that things will work out OK in the end.

The Burned concern me most. GIC and bond yields are so terrible these days that it makes it very hard for those investors to achieve their financial objectives. A couple in their fifties today with $150,000 in savings, and the ability to add $10,000 per year to their savings, will accumulate only $470,000 in fifteen years if they achieve a GIC-like return of 4%. That's likely to provide a safe annual income of less than $30,000 before inflation. I believe that most of us hope for more than that in our golden years.

The About-To-Be's, on the other hand, run the risk of getting burned at any time. Although equity markets do provide the best return over the long term, they do go up and down, significantly. The markets have been trending upward since the end of 2002 recovering quite nicely from the crash of 2000-2001. Three years of good markets should give one pause in considering how much longer the upward trend might last. In the event of another market correction, which is inevitable at some point, most scattered portfolios will behave as they did last time. They may see a 20% drop on the equity side, and two or three years passing till they recover and start to grow again. Do you want to see your portfolios stuck where they are for the next three years? That may be acceptable for thirty-year-olds who are years away from taking income. However, for those of us in our fifties we can't afford to delay. We are going to be depending on those portfolios pretty soon.

If we look again at the couple in their fifties, with $150,000 and $10,000 annually to invest, what does this mean to the About-To-Be's. Over the last fifteen years (1990 through 2004) the TSX averaged a return of 8.2%. Five of those years had negative returns with a 15% decline in 1990, and 13% and 12% declines in 2001 and 2002 respectively. Our couple may be fortunate enough to see growth averaging

12% on their equity investments for many years, but if there are two or three years of 10% or more declines, particularly if it happens in the earlier years, the ending value is drastically affected. If that couple had bought and held a fully diversified portfolio of TSX stocks with $10,000 extra annual savings over the past fifteen years, and if they had earned the market returns averaging 8.2%, they would now have $790,000, which could generate a safe income of about $47,000 per year. This is a much better than the "Burned" investors making only GIC returns, but the Cardinal Rules point to a still better and safer way.

REACHING THE MILLION-DOLLAR RETIREMENT

Following the Cardinal Rules it is still possible for that same couple to reach their million-dollar retirement goal. This would require an average return of 10.5% over the fifteen years. Impossible with GICs, unlikely with an over-diversified, multi-fund approach, but very achievable following the Cardinal approach. Even if they have entered their fifties, it's not too late for our example couple to retire as millionaires.

If you think back to Cardinal Capital's past twelve years, what did they do differently from what most of the About-to-Be's do?

- The Cardinal Rules lead to more concentrated, safer investments, not a broad basket of equities as diversified as the index.
- The Cardinal Rules receive and reinvest high, growing dividend yields.
- The Cardinal Rules constantly re-evaluate each holding looking for potential strategic weakness, divesting on expected long-term problems and investing on publicized short-term weakness.

Consequently, if our couple had followed the Cardinal Rules of

Investing for only the last twelve years, their portfolio would have grown to about $1,119,000, which could safely produce an ongoing annual income of about $61,000.

MAKING IT HAPPEN

If you're saying, "I like it. I want to do it. But What do I do, right now? How do I make this happen?" then now is the time to act.

First, for you Type A's who want to take a stab at this running-a-personal-portfolio thing, refer to Appendix II, where I provide details on how you can get started. But what about the rest of us who have other things we prefer to do with our time than scouring the stock pages and digging into corporate financial statements? Remember Tim's comment (which I strongly endorse) that, like many things, doing it right requires a true passion for doing it. What if we don't have that passion? What about those of us who want to invest like the rich, who want to be in control of directing our investments, but want to use professionals to do the work?

If you have no financial advisor at this point in time, it's past time to find one. A financial advisor that you trust works wonders in terms of helping you organize your thoughts, develop a plan for your financial future and in filtering out much of the noise that the financial services industry is capable of generating. Advisors with a CFP (Certified Financial Planner) designation have studied and achieved some proficiency in the tax and investment areas that you need. I suggest you be cautious in considering advisors employed by entities that produce their own financial products. Try to judge whether they are truly independent in determining what to recommend to you rather than influenced to recommend their house product. With an obvious bias, I can direct you to the Value Partners website (www.vpinvestments.ca) for a list of advisors who already understand and endorse the Cardinal Rules.

For those who already have a financial advisor, your action

plan should start with your advisor. But remember, he or she is an advisor. You are the client and, if you are going to invest like the rich, you need to understand and direct your own financial plan, and not allow it to be directed by an outsider. Begin by getting an understanding of what your current situation is. You can start by gathering up your financial information. Do you have investments other than through your financial advisor, at credit unions or banks? (You might ask yourself why this has occurred. Did you not trust your advisor or did you find some great deal you couldn't pass up?) Total up your investments and sort them into GICs, bonds (or bond funds) and equities. This will give you a sense of how your assets are currently allocated. Calculate how much is foreign and how much is Canadian. Estimate how much wealth your investments have made over the past few years. Note that a good advisor will have already done this for you and should regularly inform you of these facts. Therefore, if you feel you can't determine this on your own, get your advisor to do it for you.

Once you have a sense of where you are, you can assess whether you are comfortable with what is happening with your portfolio or how you want to change it. Remember, as you get closer to taking income from your portfolio, your risk is greater if your portfolio is less balanced. Similarly, if you expect to be taking your income in Canadian dollars, your currency risk is greater with more foreign equities in your investments. If you've already got lots of wealth or if you expect to live fairly cheaply in retirement – then lucky you! You can afford to be more balanced and take on less risk, while forgoing some potential return. Don't be shy about doing exactly that. Remember, success in investing is making what you need, not making the most you can. A Cardinal sin is getting greedy!

This process of assessing your current situation should involve your financial advisor. If you can let them know how you hope to live in retirement, they can help you quantify how much you need to save and grow before then in order to achieve your goal. They can give you a sense of an appropriate asset allocation for your situation and they can advise you on minimizing tax effects as you go forward.

This is also the time to broach the subject of the Cardinal Rules with your advisor. It may well be that your advisor is solidly on side philosophically with the Rules and has ideas about how to access money managers who can put them into practice for you. She or he may even be eager to use Tim Burt and the Value Partners pools. If your advisor is unaware of the Cardinal Rules and principles, loan them this book and ask him or her to read at least Chapter 3 so that you can discuss it with them. There are other large-cap value managers out there who approximate Tim's use of the Cardinal Rules, although I have yet to see many with Tim's strategic insight. If your advisor has alternative suggestions, investigate them and compare track records. Look at the holdings of the manager. Get your advisor to show you how the holdings fit the Cardinal Rules. It is important that you determine whether the proposed alternative has a low volatility, since as we discussed, that should be a primary criterion for investors our age.

Given the relatively lower volatility of portfolios using the Cardinal Rules, and considering the issue of over-diversification (Rule #5), you should not be too concerned about using Cardinal-type portfolios for a majority, or even all, of your assets – considering, of course, the Stay Balanced mandate of Rule #11. Remember that diversifying too much can dilute your returns and increase your risk. The Value Partners Foreign Equity and Canadian Income pools can give you diversification among asset classes, without watering down returns or approximating market volatility like larger, more diverse investment pools might.

Get your advisor to put together a plan that fits your asset allocation profile and that has a large commitment to Cardinal-style funds. Don't postpone the meeting to execute the plan. Get your advisor to put together the plan, and then you make sure it gets executed. It's not too late if you start now!

The Magic of Dividend Growth
Royal Bank of Canada
(1993 – 2005)

In Chapter 4, I described how common shares in the Royal Bank of Canada had been such a solid investment for the Cardinal Rules Canadian portfolios. A wonderful feature of these shares, like others we wish to focus on, has been the steady growth of their dividends. This appendix presents detailed spreadsheets that demonstrate the value of dividends, the value of dividend growth and the value of dividend re-investment in a portfolio of Canadian equity. They show how an investment in the shares in Royal Bank have grown in value as the dividends grew, and how an investment would have behaved taking the dividends as income, or re-investing them in more shares. While the discussion is somewhat theoretical, in that there are practical difficulties in buying small share amounts and fractional shares, the principle of buying and reinvesting in growing dividends is shown to be very compelling.

Figure I-1 in this appendix shows the share price on dividend dates and the dividend payment history for the Royal Bank of Canada common shares from May 31, 1993 to May 31, 2005. This discussion assumes a $10,000 purchase of common shares on May 31, 1993, which at a price of $28.50 per share, results in a purchase of 350.877

Figure I-1

Royal Bank of Canada (Common Shares-RY)
Dividend and Price History

Date	Dividend Payment (per share)	Share Price (Actual)
31-May-93		28.50
24-Aug-93	0.145	28.12
24-Nov-93	0.145	26.38
24-Feb-94	0.145	29.38
24-May-94	0.145	27.76
24-Aug-94	0.145	29.50
24-Nov-94	0.145	29.12
24-Feb-95	0.145	28.26
24-May-95	0.145	30.50
24-Aug-95	0.145	29.88
24-Nov-95	0.155	31.26
23-Feb-96	0.155	31.14
24-May-96	0.170	32.86
23-Aug-96	0.170	35.00
22-Nov-96	0.170	46.66
24-Feb-97	0.185	54.60
23-May-97	0.185	60.06
22-Aug-97	0.195	62.20
24-Nov-97	0.195	80.86
24-Feb-98	0.210	82.86
22-May-98	0.210	88.06
24-Aug-98	0.230	66.40
24-Nov-98	0.230	78.36
24-Feb-99	0.230	75.56
21-May-99	0.230	69.40
24-Aug-99	0.240	67.20
24-Nov-99	0.240	65.90
24-Feb-00	0.270	59.96
24-May-00	0.270	78.40
24-Aug-00	0.300	85.86
24-Nov-00	0.300	47.85 *
23-Feb-01	0.330	45.75
24-May-01	0.330	49.83
24-Aug-01	0.360	50.90
23-Nov-01	0.360	48.80
22-Feb-02	0.360	47.71
24-May-02	0.380	56.90
23-Aug-02	0.380	54.05
22-Nov-02	0.400	57.72
24-Feb-03	0.400	57.14
23-May-03	0.430	60.83
22-Aug-03	0.430	59.31
24-Nov-03	0.460	64.20
24-Feb-04	0.460	65.49
21-May-04	0.520	59.98
24-Aug-04	0.520	62.72
24-Nov-04	0.520	61.85
24-Feb-05	0.550	67.00
24-May-05	0.550	76.80
31-May-05		75.00

* One-for-One Share Dividend, October 2000

shares. Note that although the share price climbs over the life of the investment, there are declines in share price from time to time. In particular you can see that by Nov. 24, 1993, the share price dropped 7.5% to $26.38 from the May 31st price. Being a common share and despite its healthy dividend, the share price does fluctuate, with declines as well as increases. Also you may note that the share price drops drastically from over $85 in August 2000 to less than $48 in November 2000. This is because during that time the number of shares was doubled, with each shareholder receiving free a second share for each share already owned. This had the effect of halving the share price at that time, but doubling the dividend received by each shareholder.

You can see that the share price on May 31st of 1993 was $28.50 and that the dividend rate for the last two quarters of 1993 was $0.145 per share per quarter. This represented an annual dividend of $0.58 per share (4 x $0.145) for a dividend yield of 2.04% (0.58 / 28.50), which is not overly exciting in and of itself. However, note that the dividend rate has grown and at May 24 2005 stood at $0.55 per share per quarter. The August 2005 dividend rate (not shown) was increased to $0.61 or $2.44 per year. Since the one-for-one share dividend paid in 2000 means that every share owned in1993 received another share, then each share owned from 1993 effectively now earns $4.88 in dividends ($2.44 x 2) each year. This amount represents a yield of over 17% on the original purchase price of $28.50 (4.88 / 28.50 = 17.12%), which easily beats the yield available on bonds or GICs.

A growing stream of dividends is a wonderful thing, especially when you can realize a yield of 17%. But the wonder of dividend-paying stocks is that if dividends increase, by and large, the share price goes up! You can see that the May 1993 share price of $28.50 had increased to $75.00 by 31 May 2005, but of course, that does not reflect the fact that every one share turned into two. The original

Figure I-2

Royal Bank of Canada

Dividend Reinvestment Activity

$10,000 Investment in May 1993

Date	Shares Owned	Dividends Received	Share Price	Shares Bought
24-Aug-93	350.877	$50.88	$28.12	1.809
24-Nov-93	352.686	$51.14	$26.38	1.939
24-Feb-94	354.625	$51.42	$29.38	1.750
24-May-94	356.375	$51.67	$27.76	1.861
24-Aug-94	358.237	$51.94	$29.50	1.761
24-Nov-94	359.998	$52.20	$29.12	1.793
24-Feb-95	361.790	$52.46	$28.26	1.856
24-May-95	363.646	$52.73	$30.50	1.729
24-Aug-95	365.375	$52.98	$29.88	1.773
24-Nov-95	367.148	$56.91	$31.26	1.820
23-Feb-96	368.969	$57.19	$31.14	1.837
24-May-96	370.805	$63.04	$32.86	1.918
23-Aug-96	372.724	$63.36	$35.00	1.810
22-Nov-96	374.534	$63.67	$46.66	1.365
24-Feb-97	375.899	$69.54	$54.60	1.274
23-May-97	377.172	$69.78	$60.06	1.162
22-Aug-97	378.334	$73.78	$62.20	1.186
24-Nov-97	379.520	$74.01	$80.86	0.915
24-Feb-98	380.435	$79.89	$82.86	0.964
22-May-98	381.400	$80.09	$88.06	0.910
24-Aug-98	382.309	$87.93	$66.40	1.324
24-Nov-98	383.633	$88.24	$78.36	1.126
24-Feb-99	384.759	$88.49	$75.56	1.171
21-May-99	385.931	$88.76	$69.40	1.279
24-Aug-99	387.210	$92.93	$67.20	1.383
24-Nov-99	388.592	$93.26	$65.90	1.415
24-Feb-00	390.008	$105.30	$59.96	1.756
24-May-00	391.764	$105.78	$78.40	1.349
24-Aug-00	393.113	$117.93	$85.86	1.374
24-Nov-00	788.973	$236.69	$47.85	4.947
23-Feb-01	793.920	$261.99	$45.75	5.727
24-May-01	799.646	$263.88	$49.83	5.296
24-Aug-01	804.942	$289.78	$50.90	5.693
23-Nov-01	810.635	$291.83	$48.80	5.980
22-Feb-02	816.615	$293.98	$47.71	6.162
24-May-02	822.777	$312.66	$56.90	5.495
23-Aug-02	828.272	$314.74	$54.05	5.823
22-Nov-02	834.095	$333.64	$57.72	5.780
24-Feb-03	839.876	$335.95	$57.14	5.879
23-May-03	845.755	$363.67	$60.83	5.979
22-Aug-03	851.733	$366.25	$59.31	6.175
24-Nov-03	857.909	$394.64	$64.20	6.147
24-Feb-04	864.056	$397.47	$65.49	6.069
21-May-04	870.125	$452.46	$59.98	7.544
24-Aug-04	877.668	$456.39	$62.72	7.277
24-Nov-04	884.945	$460.17	$61.85	7.440
24-Feb-05	892.385	$490.81	$67.00	7.326
24-May-05	899.711	$494.84	$76.80	6.443
31-May-05	906.154			

$28.50 investment is actually worth $150.00 now ($75 x 2). What kind of bond or GIC gives you a return while you own it, a return that goes up eight-fold (from 2% to 17%) and yet is still worth 525% more now than when you bought it?! Dividend growth investments are ideally suited for enhancing the returns of the retired or near retired investor.

Of course there is a way to earn even more. For the investor who doesn't need income, they can always realize the wonder of compounding. This is possible because if the dividends don't need to be taken for income, they can be reinvested into more shares instead. As you can see from Figure I-2, a $10,000 investment in 1993 bought 350.877 shares which earned dividends in each quarter of $50.88, or for the year, $203.51   Using the market share prices that existed at the dividend dates, it can be calculated that these dividend amounts could have been used to buy 7.39 additional shares over the first four quarters. (1.809 + 1.939 + 1.750 + 1.861=7.39) Ownership of more shares increases the amount of total dividends received and so on, so that by August 24, 2000, you would now own 393.113 shares (Figure I–2),

Figure I-3

The Magic of Dividend Re-Investment
$10,000 Investment in Royal Bank - Common (RY)
31-May-93

Date	Dividends Received on Original Purchase	Investment Value if Dividends Not Reinvested	Investment Value if Dividends Reinvested
Jun 93 - May 94	$203.51	$9,782	$9,988
Jun 94 - May 95	$203.51	$10,614	$11,053
Jun 95 - May 96	$219.30	$11,491	$12,207
Jun 96 - May 97	$249.12	$21,018	$22,662
Jun 97 - May 98	$284.21	$31,228	$34,026
Jun 98 - May 99	$322.81	$24,070	$26,563
Jun 99 - May 00	$357.89	$27,316	$30,604
Jun 00 - May 01	$778.95	$34,344	$39,394
Jun 01 - May 02	$1,024.56	$41,123	$48,537
Jun 02 - May 03	$1,129.82	$41,326	$50,159
Jun 03 - May 04	$1,312.28	$41,446	$51,835
Jun 04 - May 05	$1,501.75	$52,632	$67,962

and be receiving $117.93 per quarter in dividends, an annual return of 4.7% on our original investment of $10,000. This dividend would buy an additional 1.374 shares so that in November of 2000, we would receive an additional 394.49 shares in the stock dividend of that quarter.

Figure I–3 shows that carrying this activity forward to May 31, 2005 would have increased the value of $10,000 to $67,962 or 680%. This is more than $15,000 (or 29%) more than the investment would be worth if you took the dividends as income over this twelve-year period. This represents a total compound return of 17.3% per year.

Investing in growing dividends is a beautiful thing.

Going It Alone:
Tips For The Do-It-Yourselfer

If you believe that you have the mindset, knowledge and experience to start practicing the Cardinal Rules on your own, I wish you luck. This book will have given you a good idea of what the Cardinal Rules are all about and this appendix will lay out a few first steps and data sources for you to consider.

Before you buy a stock I would recommend you start your search by getting a copy of a recent Saturday edition of the Report on Business section of the Globe and Mail (assuming you will primarily or firstly focus on Canadian equities). Look for the Toronto stock listings (not the Venture exchange) and go through the listings looking at the columns headed by "yld" (yield) and "p/e ratio" (price/earnings ratio). Yield is the calculated dividend yield based on the previous day's closing price and the sum of the dividends paid in the last twelve months. This number can be a little deceiving in that the dividend amount used is not necessarily what you want to use. What you really want is the current dividend amount, not the total for the last twelve months. If a company has recently changed its dividend rate, a yield based on the last twelve months will not be very useful. If a company has cut its rate (not too common) then the printed yield will be too high. If a company has raised its rate, its printed yield will actually be lower than its real yield.

Likewise, the p/e ratio is based on the earnings most recently reported by the company. Again these numbers are not normalized and may include extraordinary or unusual earnings that should not be in a normalized figure. Therefore, remember that you are dealing with raw computerized data, unprocessed or filtered by a human who knows the story behind the numbers.

Still, you have to start somewhere and this set of figures is easily available, consistent, and well-presented. One of the aspects of running your own portfolio is that almost all figures have to be verified and assessed to determine their real meaning. What you are doing at this step is looking for companies that might fit the Cardinal Rules bill for selection. At this stage, you are not actually buying those you find, but it is one way to start preparing a list to review further.

At this point look for high values in the yld column and low values in the p/e ratio column. Make a list of say, fifty to one hundred stocks that have attractive attributes. The more you select as this point the more company specific data you will have to dig into and evaluate. However, the longer the list, the less likely you will miss out on a good company such as one that has raised its dividend lately (so that its yield is understated) or one that has a large negative impact on its earnings from an extraordinary or unusual event (thus overstating its p/e).

Now comes the hard part. For each company you have identified, go to the Investment Relations section of their website (or go to www.sedar.com) and access the last five years of financial statements and annual reports. Also get the latest Annual Information Form filed by the company. Remember under Cardinal Rules #1 and #2 in Chapter 3, I discussed a number of ratios and issues of a Quality company that should be evaluated, including debt/equity ratios, current assets and notes regarding the long-term debt. You may want to review some of the material in Chapter 3 again as you go through the statements and data for the companies you have identified. Of course you will check out the earnings growth rates, the dividend payout ratios and the dividend growth rates, hopefully even preparing five year historical data sheets so that you can see trends in the above and in other important ratios. You will use these history sheets as criteria for decisions, but some pieces of data will raise questions in your mind. Get the answers to those questions. Become a detective. Learn why the trends are occurring as they are. And remember that while the numbers in themselves are important, even more important is that you learn everything you can about the companies. You are trying to become as familiar with them as you are with your own finances.

The management discussions in the annual reports will identify market and competitive trends that management thinks are important. Consider their arguments and the industry, from what you know of it. Do you agree with the issues and solutions and strategies that management presents? Are there issues that are being ignored? There is another wonderful resource for getting explanations to questions that arise. That is the companies themselves. Most large public companies have an Investor Relations department that is there to answer investor questions about the company. The websites and annual reports usually provide the numbers, addresses and sometimes names of people you can contact. To properly use this resource you should not phone or email with one question at a time. Complete as much of your trend sheets as you can and identify all the questions on each company that you can. If you have questions about the strategy or industry trends that you cannot satisfactorily address, have them ready too. Have your questions written down before you call, or include them in the email. Take notes as you converse so that you can remember all the important points of the discussion. Also remember that you are communicating with a paid employee of the company.

Their job, in many ways, is to present their company in the best possible light. Be skeptical where necessary, but do not argue with the person. They cannot change corporate policy. As an insider they may share their opinions, thoughts or attitudes about their company with you, but this is more likely to occur if you strike up a friendly, knowledgeable conversation than if you argue or dispute their every point. (Think of Peter Falk as Detective Columbo!!)

This process may take a month or two, but will gradually result in names falling off the list. Analysing the published numbers alone may help you winnow your initial list down to 40 or 50 names. It should also result in identifying 10 or 20 companies that really look attractive to you. Now that you have this short list you have to take your analysis up to the next level. "Take it up a notch," as Emeril would say.

Going through the management reports in the Annual Reports will start you thinking about the state of the industry each company is in. Next take that one step further by identifying each company's competitors. Statistics Canada industry reports will list companies reporting in each industry and this may help identify competitors. These reports (at least for old-line traditional industries) will also show total industry sales, employees, number of plants, etc. This might help to give you a better sense of industry trends. Many industries have a trade journal or magazine that reports on events and participants in the industry. This too can be invaluable in identifying industry players, new trends, personnel changes and corporate activities. Google the industry on the internet and see if you can find such trade journals or look into the periodical index at your library. While you are googling, check out all the news stories on the company over the past 12 months. These are often available on financial sites such as Yahoo or Globeinvest. Remember you are a detective trying to find out everything you can about the industry and the company. Some professional analysts have been known to park outside plant gates and count trucks in order to see how business is faring. Others have been known to frequent drinking establishments known to be haunts of company employees in order to eavesdrop on company gossip. It is not really necessary for the retail investor to go to these extremes, but these stories indicate the mindset that you should have when investigating the target companies in which you are considering investing your hard-earned money.

The object is to try to understand current trends and factors in the industry. Think about the practicality and the potential of the companies you have listed in relation to their competitors and in the context of their industry. From the sectors your companies are in, try to identify those sectors that appear to have long-term promise. Are the companies on your list Quality companies that appear to have strong dividend growth potential based on their earnings growth and dividend payout? Is one of the competitors a better prospect in the industry for you to choose as an investment? If so, get their annual reports and check out their numbers.

Establishing your shortlist is not a simple process. Don't be surprised if it takes you six to twelve months to be really comfortable with and knowledgeable about ten to fifteen companies, either from your initial list or others that you have added as a result of your research.

When you feel you are close to identifying Quality companies that you wish to own a piece of, start following the prices at which they trade on the market. Get a sense of what daily volume is in relation to what you want to buy. Are prices near their 52-week high or the low? Are the headlines good or bad? Are there new research reports out there touting their merits? Has that activity inflated the price? Is there bad news released about an industrial accident, a lawsuit or missed earnings? If that doesn't substantially impact the Quality nature of the firm and its competitive position, maybe it has temporarily knocked the market price back and you can get a good deal. (Remember, it's a market of stocks, not a stock market!) Pull the trigger and make your buys whenever you are comfortable that you are getting good Value. Remember to trade in regular block size lots, not in odd lots, in order to keep your trading costs efficient. Consider whether the company has a Dividend Reinvestment Program, and whether you want to participate in that.

After you have made your purchases, continue to watch for news about your holdings, about the industries they are in and about their competitors. Constantly ask: "Is this still a Quality industry and a Quality company?" Remember, while going through this process ignore the emotion in the headlines and think and act strategically. Which good companies are in a good position to prosper in their markets over the next few years; over the next decade? These are the candidates that meet the criteria of the Cardinal Rules. Find a small but diversified basket of these companies, watch them and, with luck, you too will retire wealthy!

INDEX